I HAD NO MEANS

TO SHOUT!

D1506545

I HAD NO MEANS TO SHOUT!

by

Mary Jane Gray Hale

and

Charles Martel Hale, Jr.

ISBN: 1-58500-401-4

1stBooks – rev. 1/24/00

About the Book

This book is about hope and love and the undaunted courage of the human spirit crying to be heard. It is a story about our son, Charles, who was trapped for thirty-six years in a body which could not speak.

Believed to be severely or profoundly mentally retarded, unable to show emotion at will by facial expression, Charles kept the faith. He prayed that the day would come when God would give him a means of allowing his parents and the rest of the world to know that he was cognitive with a heart full of love for God and Man. He wanted to be ready and so he listened, learned and observed life as it is lived by verbal people.

When the technique of facilitated communication was offered to him, Charles was ready. Slowly, he embraced it fully and the pages which follow are a saga of rebirth and a celebration of life.

Charles' story is not unique. There are many other nonverbal individuals out there just waiting for people to reach out to them and bring a little light into their otherwise dormant, isolated lives. Being human, there is an innate desire to communicate. When this is blocked, the result is an overwhelming feeling of inadequacy. It prevents them from entering what Charles refers to as "the real world."

INDEX

"I HAD NO MEANS TO SHOUT!"

My dream of life has come to be;
My hope has come to me.
I can call to someone through my hands
And all the world can see.
If I can keep this dream alive,
I might be known throughout
To sail the oceans and sail the skies
With my all inspiring shout.
My heart is full.
My hope is great.
My story I will tell.
My thoughts come rapidly to mind
And my feelings tumble out.
My eyes are words.
My hands are thoughts.
My heart is full of fear
As I begin my journey through my words
To teach the world the things my heart will tell about.
If I can impart to you what I know to be the truth,
My mind is better than I dreamed to wish
And soon you will know about
The things my heart has wished to say,
But had no means to shout.

Charles Martel Hale, Jr.
1993

DEDICATION

This book is lovingly dedicated to Dr. Douglas Biklen of Syracuse University, Syracuse, New York, who changed my life and the lives of so many other nonverbal people when he brought Rosemary Crossley's technique of Facilitated Communication to the United States in 1989.

Charles Martel Hale, Jr.

The following analogy was written to Charles by Elizabeth Lawrence, the actress, who was working with him, when he was a young, hyperactive boy, in an A.H.R.C. school program, in Queens, New York:

"FOR CHARLES -
TALL, SLIM AND FAIR,
SHREWD AND QUICK,
WITH HANDS LIKE BIRDS
AND HAIR LIKE DOWN.
SPARROW AND SEAGULL
POISED FOR FLIGHT.
TAKE OFF, SWEET BOY,
INTO BRIGHTER TOMORROWS!"

ELIZABETH

...AND HE DID!

INTRODUCTION

This book is about hope and love and the undaunted courage of the human spirit crying to be heard. It is a story about our son, Charles, who was trapped for thirty-six years in a body which could not speak.

Believed to be severely or profoundly mentally retarded, unable to show emotion at will by facial expression, Charles kept the faith. He prayed that the day would come when God would give him a means of allowing his parents and the rest of the world to know that he was cognitive with a heart full of love for God and Man. He wanted to be ready and so he listened, learned and observed life as it is lived by verbal people.

When the technique of Facilitated Communication was offered to him, Charles was ready. Slowly, he embraced it fully and the pages which follow are a saga of rebirth and a celebration of life.

Charles' story is not unique. There are many other nonverbal individuals out there just waiting for people to reach out to them and bring a little light into their otherwise dormant, isolated lives. Being human, there is an innate desire to communicate. When this is blocked, the result is an overwhelming feeling of inadequacy. It prevents them from entering what Charles refers to as "the real world."

As Charles' mother, I am the primary author and coordinator of the story which is to follow. Throughout the pages of our book, there will be many comments by Charles who will be verbally expressing himself through the technique of facilitated communication. The reader will see much of his work as he originally typed it; however, in order to spare the reader the task of having to slowly read through the many typographical errors which occur, many of Charles' communications will have been typographically corrected with punctuation and capitals added. The only reason that so many typographical errors remain is to allow the reader to see how most communications from people using facilitated communication will appear. They are not skilled typists. The disabled individual, the speaker, will have his/her hand supported by the facilitator, the receiver, thus allowing the speaker to use his/her index finger to reach out and point to the different keys of the typewriter, computer or letter board. The facilitator steadies the hand and gives emotional, but not guiding, support to the speaker. Between each letter, good technique calls for the facilitator to pull back the hand or arm of the speaker, thus allowing the speaker to then reach out to the next letter, thereby reducing the possibility of perseveration and facilitator influence.

In the second chapter of our book, the story of Charles' breakthrough on facilitated communication will be related by a newspaper article appearing in 1993, in the Winchester Star, here in Winchester, Virginia. The one criticism I have of the article, Charles Hale Is Silent No More, is the statement that my husband, Martel, and I did not care whether or not Charles was ever able to type independently. This is not true as, even in our euphoria, we realized that one of Charles' top priorities should be working toward independent typing. In order for a verbally impaired mind to be truly free of imprisonment, it is important to work toward eliminating the need for a facilitator. Whether or not Charles is ever able to reach his goal of typing independence, what he has to say to us is both enlightening, thought provoking and worthy of attention.

Charles' comments in the book will be shown in quotations. The story begins with the above mentioned newspaper article, moves back in time to the early years of his life in Fresh Meadows, New York, and returns again to Winchester, where our family moved in 1979 and remains to date. Charles was 22 years old when we moved to Winchester, but his verbal breakthrough via facilitated communication did not occur until he had reached the age of 36, when Charles' father, Martel, and I were first blessed with the opportunity to really begin to know our beautiful son named Charles.

ACKNOWLEDGMENTS

We would like to express our sincere appreciation to both past and present staff members of the following facilities who are currently providing a lifeline of services to Charles, here, in Winchester, Virginia:

Northwestern Workshop (Robert C. Romagna, Director) (Former Directors: Susan Dawkins Ireland; Pia Crandell) which provides both in-facility and community based employment opportunities for adults with disabilities, with the goal being to help individuals find employment of their choice.

Grafton School (Robert Stieg, Headmaster), a private, not-for-profit, nationally recognized leader in the education of individuals who have serious cognitive, communication and behavioral disorders. Grafton's mission is to assist individuals, whose options are limited, by providing services that lead to their maximum independence and community inclusion.

A special "thank you" to the following people who have added their comments in our book and to whom we are indebted for so much more: Nancy Bagatell, Connie Clem, Lincoln Grigsby, Joan Mariah, Susan Utt and Lynne Van Evera..

A word of appreciation to other friends who have acted as "sounding boards" and advisors during the writing of this book: Phil and Joan Bettendorf, Charles O. and Elaine Davis, Lorry Fridinger, Vera Pistel, Geraldine Roper, Gerard Seuferling, Peggy Shamblin and Lucita Stowe.

A heartfelt word of appreciation to both past and present members of Charles' Grafton residential staff on Packer Street (House Director, James Bowman). They are as follows: Jaimie Belford, Yvonne Brant, Joshua Cintron, Amy Clem, Phyllis Henrichon, Roseann Hill, Todd Miller, Jennifer Shaffer, Bill Shore, Mike Vandervelde and Duane Wilson.

We would be remiss if we did not express our sincere gratitude to other Workshop and Grafton School professionals who have given special help and moral support to Charles throughout the years. They are: Stephen Beck, Karen Berlin,

Connie Clem, Leona Farris, Julie Hayes, Reynold Hicks, Sean Hilleary, Betty Holland, Susan Dawkins Ireland, Vera Pistel, Bob and Jean Sowers, Tricia Stiles, Susan Utt, Lynne Van Evera and Sherry Wotring.

A very special "thank you" to our friend, Ginger Spiker, who saved the day by coming forth and providing her capable secretarial skills in the conversion of our manuscript, from the word processor to the computer.

Our sincere gratitude to the staff of Northwestern Community Services, Inc., and especially, to Adele McGeechy who has been Charles' case manager for several years.

Dear friends, one and all.

And, lastly, our love and appreciation to my darling husband and Charles' father, Martel, without whose love, encouragement and support, we probably would not have had the heart to have attempted to write our story in the first place. Daddy, we love you very much.

Chapter One

Facilitated Communication

Facilitated Communication: Description

The following description of Facilitated Communication is from the office of Dr. Douglas Biklen, Division of Special Education & Rehabilitation, Syracuse University, Syracuse, New York:

Facilitated communication is a means of "facilitating" expression by people who either do not talk or do not talk clearly. Rosemary Crossley, an Australian educator and founder of the DEAL Communication Centre in Melbourne, is the originator of the method. She believes that for people with autism and other communication disabilities, the problem of communication may not be essentially cognitive but is, rather, a kind of apraxia. That is, many people with developmental disabilities who have major communication problems have trouble with expression; they cannot put their ideas or intentions into spoken words. But with facilitation, these people can point to letters and thus construct words, phrases and sentences. The method involves initial hand-over-hand and/or arm support, pulling the hand back after each selection, slowing down the movements, assistance in isolating the index finger, verbal reassurances, and encouragement. Over time, the physical support can be faded back completely or to just a hand on the shoulder.

The Facilitated Communication Controversy

Since the introduction of this technique into the United States by Dr. Douglas Biklen of Syracuse University, facilitated communication has been a God-send to many totally nonverbal or speech impaired individuals, some of whom might be literally locked away and imprisoned within their own bodies with no means of communication with their fellow man except through the means of gesturing and body language. Many of the developmentally disabled are so neurologically impaired that, until the introduction of facilitated communication into their lives, they have been virtually untestable as to their intellectual capacity; therefore, when finally presented with the opportunity to enable the world to see that they are cognitive individuals, skepticism became a factor with which these individuals, their families, and professional advocates had to contend. To hear the words of these disabled people coming through via facilitated communication, showing a full spectrum of individual intellectual capacities and articulation, after having been believed to be so intellectually impaired all of their lives, was more than many people were able to understand and accept. As time went on, professionals in the field began to conduct testing to try to prove the validation of facilitated communication and its users. For many reasons, not all of these attempts at validation were successful, due to the emotional and physical vulnerability of these motor impaired people who, in many cases, resented having to prove themselves in the first place. Qualitative testing, rather than objective, quantitative testing has proved to be the most reliable less invasive validation method of testing disabled individuals using facilitated communication. For positive testing results, I refer the reader to Contested Words---Contested Science by Douglas Biklen and Donald Cardinal.

For many nonverbal people, their neuromotor disturbance is so acute that writing, signing or other augmentative modes of communication are not feasible and facilitated communication may be their only method of verbally freeing themselves. Rosemary Crossley, in her book titled Facilitated Communication Training, on page 7, sums it up very well as follows: "Facilitated communication training has excited attention because the communication produced with facilitation is unexpected in both style and content, and challenges previous assumptions about the language skills of specific groups, especially people with autism. The most important contribution facilitated communication training could make to the field of nonspeech communication would be to bring about the reevaluation of individuals with severe communication impairments who are labeled as intellectually impaired, and a reexamination of the methods used to assess these individuals. Detailed neuromotor assessment of all infants with significant speech delays and early intervention by speech/language pathologists and physical therapists could eradicate the need for facilitated communication training within a generation. In the meantime, the findings that led to facilitated communication training should add further impetus to research into the neurological links between speech and hand function."

In addition to the scientific controlled testing which has taken place, and continues, with regard to facilitated communication, there are other qualitative ways for parents and professionals to satisfy themselves as to who is doing the speaking in the communication process. Validation may also be obtained by message passing by a third party, through the speaker, where the facilitator is unaware of the content of the message, thereby eliminating the possibility of the message being the facilitator's. Also, a speaker's vocabulary, pattern and unique irregularities of spelling and articulating with different facilitators gives credence to the message being the speaker's rather than the facilitator's. I have always felt that a strong indication of the messages being Charles' rather than a facilitator's is the fact that his loving nature, in addition to his lack of intimidation in being able to tell people how he feels about them, comes through in these communications. Wouldn't it be wonderful if we could all feel able to express ourselves, so freely, without feeling so vulnerable? Charles seems to have no such inhibitions. Also, obviously, one of the most validating factors for the users of facilitated communication is the change in their behavior. The improvement in their self-stimulating, perseverating patterns, the unspoken communication through their eye contact, and their newfound feelings of self -confidence are often very apparent, especially if the observer is well acquainted with their mannerisms prior to their use of facilitated communication. I remember that among the first things I noticed about Charles, after he began to communicate through facilitated communication, were the intelligent, knowing glances which came through from the beginning. It was almost as if a light had been turned on in his life and he was imploring us to see.

Facilitated communication is, indeed, a phenomenon which may lend itself to misuse; however, just as with any other method of communication, the disabled individuals, whose sad and lonely worlds have been partially opened, surely deserve to be heard without the constant hassle of having to prove that they are doing the speaking. Can you imagine the frustration of being nonverbal most of your life, finally being given a means of expressing yourself, only to end up having to prove to the world that what you are saying is actually coming from you? It is as though you just cannot win for losing! Instead of embracing these people, being happy for them and wanting them to live out the remainder of their isolated lives more peacefully and with as much happiness as their disability will allow, they are, in many instances, not being given this right. Life, at best, is short and they have surely paid their dues. Shouldn't they be given the benefit of the doubt?

Since the beginning of its use, facilitated communication has brought to mind many questions concerning its authenticity, both by the skeptics as well as the proponents of the technique. Some of the most frequently asked questions are as follow:

1.   How is it possible for individuals, who have previously been unable to verbally even ask a question before being introduced to facilitated communication, to suddenly be able to display varying degrees of cognition and learning skills which have previously been thought to be acquired by having been taught the conventional way?

2.   How much facilitator influence is there in a message being sent by the speaker?

4

3.   Why are some parents and educators so successful in acting as facilitators with the users of facilitated communication while, still, others are unsuccessful in their attempts to facilitate?

4.   What are the factors which come into play to allow a nonverbal individual to speak through the use of facilitated communication?   Also, why with some facilitators and not others?

5.   In cases of sexual accusations having been brought by a speaker, who is doing the accusing, the speaker or the facilitator?

6.   When there is telepathic content in a message, is this really "facilitated communication" or is it "spiritual communication" resulting from poor technique?

7.   In a case where a telepathic message has been sent by a speaker, how much of the message, if any, is due to facilitator influence?

8.   How are some facilitated communication users able to type their messages by using their peripheral vision, a practice which does not promote "best practices" technique and the possibility of their eventual typing independence?   Why do so many facilitated communication users find it so difficult to look at the typewriter, computer or letter board?

9.   Why do some studies conclude the authenticity of facilitated communication, for some people, under certain conditions, while other studies do not indicate that validation?

From the time of the introduction of facilitated communication into the United States by Dr. Douglas Biklen, in 1989, until 1993, it perhaps was making the greatest impact into the lives of the nonverbal developmentally disabled and was often embraced by both parents and professionals in the field. Probably the two greatest setbacks with the progress of facilitated communication, to date, have been the sexual accusations being brought by several users of the technique and the extremely biased and unfair handling of the Prisoners of Silence Frontline Report, in October, 1993.

In an interview with TASH's Newsletter Editor, Sheryl Ball, following the October 19, 1993 Frontline Report, Dr. Biklen discussed some of the false accusations, as well as several important omissions, which Jon Palfreman, the producer of the

Frontline Report, presented in this media coverage. They are as follow: "Frontline told its viewers that autism involves brain damage, but failed to interview the leading pediatric neurologists whose work demonstrates that the anomalies are subcortical, not in the cortex where higher thinking occurs.

Frontline never showed the progress that some individuals are making toward independence. Indeed, Sharisa Kochmeister is shown in the program, but isn't typing on CBS' How'd They Do That?, and Sharisa now types completely independently. She has gone from being diagnosed as severely retarded to demonstrating quite normal intelligence.

The program failed to note that Rosemary Crossley, myself, and others who have been doing research on facilitation have long discussed issues of facilitator influence and the importance of helping people work toward independence.

They decided to show footage only of people looking away from the keyboard, even though we have been clear from the start (as I noted in my article in the Harvard Educational Review, 1990) that looking at the keyboard is a requirement of the method: Frontline does not explain that someone who can have difficulty with this can improve on looking and can achieve this skill; success with this goes hand-in-hand with achieving independence.

Frontline mentioned only negative studies, systematically not letting the public know about the studies that support the finding that facilitation is an effective alternative means of communication. They distinctly avoided reporting the results from our observational research.

False claims were made on the program, stating that facilitated communication is invariably perfectly spelled and grammatically correct -- we have not found that or reported as such.

Frontline told the story of a case in which a person purportedly made an abuse allegation, but did not report the procedure that we have recommended for over a year for sorting out such claims.

There was no mention of the parents who discovered the method on their own, and who found that their children could type independently (see Margaret Eastham's 1992 book Silent words) or semi-independent typing (see particularly Oppenheim's 1974 book Teaching Methods for Autistic Children).

Frontline made no mention of the theory behind facilitation (i.e. apraxia).

There was no identification of Dr. Arthur Schawlow as a Nobel Prize Winner in Physics - as someone who knows a great deal about science and who is very critical of the recent studies that claim to discredit facilitation. Frontline failed to air his criticism of those studies."

As a parent of a severely impaired developmentally disabled son, I am appalled at the biased Frontline Report, Prisoners of silence. It is difficult to understand how anyone with a conscience could possibly allow such a one sided program to be presented, especially when it may have such repercussions to some of the most vulnerable individuals in the world, those without voices until facilitated communication.

Concerning the false, as well as the true, sexual allegations which have occurred over the years, I don't for one moment minimize what devastation these accusations have brought to families involved in such; however, not all allegations have been proven to be false once they reach the stage of litigation in the courts. It is my understanding that the allogations being brought by the disabled, in proportion to the so called "normal" population, are about the same.

Once an allegation reaches the courts, in order to provide substantial evidence that the accusation is originating with the person who uses facilitated communication to speak, a second facilitator, who is unfamiliar with the details of the allegation, may be brought in to facilitate with the speaker; if the message is the same or similar, then this would indicate that the message originates with the speaker rather than the facilitator. After that, it is then left up to the courts to decide whether the allegation is true or false. Some allegations have been proven to be true by virtue of physical examinations indicating that there was abuse.

Probably some of the strongest and most vociferous skeptics in the facilitated communication controversy are the parents or professionals who have been hurt or devastated when a sexual allegation by a facilitated communication user proves to be false. Because of the serious consequences of a false accusation, it is only human to respond with such vehemence and contempt; however, I ask the injured party to consider the consequences of being strongly belligerent against the use of facilitated communication as a lifeline to the speechless. False and hurtful accusations are made by countless non-disabled people every day that we live, but are we to deny them the right to speak? If one could hear the agony of a speechless person, as well as the joy when he/she, at long last, finds a way to communicate, perhaps he/she might reconsider giving them the benefit of the doubt. It would be wonderful if the opponents could keep an open mind even if they could never become advocates. I sincerely hope that they can find it in their hearts to hear the cries of so many who need our love and understanding. The controversy goes on and on. I pray that one day soon it will end for the multitudes who are still waiting to be heard.

Chapter Two

Charles Hale Is Silent No More

(Excerpted from Stan Hough's award-winning article in The Winchester Star on June 9, 1993)

CHARLES HALE IS SILENT NO MORE

Martel Hale remembers waving good-bye to his 3-year old son, Charles, and receiving a vacant stare in return.

Jane Hale remembers the constant assurances from her doctor that Charles was just slow in developing, to not be overly alarmed in spite of the fact that Charles had yet to make an intelligible sound well past his third birthday.

It wasn't a time to act; it was a time to wait, she was told.

Then came the seizures at 4, test upon test, and the subsequent diagnosis that Charles had suffered brain damage at birth, possibly brought on by a combination of factors, but too much time had passed to accurately determine the cause.

For the next 32 years, the Hales did what most loving parents would do and took their son to doctor after doctor; program after program. "Everything we could possibly find," Jane said.

The results were always the same, but the Hales managed to cope.

"The abnormal became normal," said Martel.

"You either get stronger or you fall apart," Jane said.

Charles hasn't spoken a word in his life. He walks normally, but because of neurological damage he has trouble controlling the muscles in his hands. When he becomes agitated or excited, his hands flutter.

His hearing is fine, and he understands directions and commands. He's been diagnosed as severely mentally retarded, "trainable" but not "educable," with a comprehension level of a 2- or 3-year old child- at least that is what the Hales had been led to believe for all these years, what they grudgingly accepted until March (1993).

As a mother would, Mrs. Hale said she always believed her son had an intelligence beyond those grim labels, beyond his listless and often sullen demeanor. And it appears that Mrs. Hale was right - right beyond her wildest dreams.

It is time for redefinition, for re-examination, for rebirth in the Hale home on Walker Street in Winchester.

After 36 years, Charles Martel Hale, Jr. can speak - not through his voice box, but through his right index finger and a computer screen or a piece of paper in a typewriter. What he has to say is lucid, at times poignant, and certainly intelligent.

"Our neighbors are calling it 'The Miracle on Walker Street,'" Martel said.

Helping Hand

What allows Charles to communicate is a controversial technique called facilitated communication. Charles cannot type without the help of a facilitator, someone to steady his hand as he types.

His primary facilitators are his mother and Julie Hayes and Susan Utt, adult education teachers at Northwestern Workshop, a training center primarily for mentally-disabled adults just across the Winchester city limits in Frederick County near Smithfield Avenue.

Utt and Hayes have been using facilitated communication for less than a year, having learned the technique from a workshop offered by Grafton School, a private, nonprofit school based in Clarke County (Virginia) for mentally disabled and disturbed children and young adults.

Julie Hunt, who runs Grafton's facilitated communication program, said recently that the school had been using the technique since 1990 and is getting, in many cases, remarkable results.

Autistic students who have severe language impairments and for the most part have traditionally been considered mentally retarded, have been communicating in cogent sentences and expressing opinions - basically displaying a full range of cognitive abilities - through facilitated communication.

"Each and every case is wonderful and exciting compared to what they could do before," Hunt said.

Facilitated communication was brought to the United States from Australia in late 1989 by Douglas Biklen, a special education and rehabilitation professor at Syracuse University.

The technique has yet to be sanctioned by major associations in the mental health and developmental disability field where it's being "derided as much as it's being embraced," Hunt said.

Skeptics believe the facilitator, either consciously or subconsciously, is guiding the student's finger to the appropriate keys.

To acknowledge otherwise would force an almost complete redefinition of long-held views on mental retardation and autism, Hunt said.

The controversy has fostered a sense of caution, a "long, hard look" at facilitated communication that isn't without its merits, she said.

"I've seen and heard of wonderful success stories that have changed lives and I've read and heard of horror stories that have destroyed lives, " Hunt said.   "It's a technique susceptible to misuse."

"There have been cases where charges of abuse were brought out through facilitated communication and then later found to be false, " Hunt said.

"Used properly with trained facilitators, the technique has tremendous potential, not only in freeing a trapped mind but in helping to properly diagnose levels of retardation and impairment in individuals who would otherwise be untestable," she said.

Hunt saw a glimpse of that potential at an international conference on facilitated communication last month in Syracuse, where a young man who had begun with facilitated communication typed independently. "There's no denying a case like that," she said.

Days of Wonder

As much as her mind tells her to be skeptical, as much as her gut tells here that it is beyond logical probability, Susan Utt said there's no denying that Charles Hale, and not herself, is choosing which keys to hit on the computer at Northwestern.

Nothing in her experience as an adult education teacher, nearly 10 years at Northwestern, prepared her for Charles' breakthrough, she said.

Up until March, she thought Charles unreachable and unresponsive. The workshop has several stages of development for its "workers." Most are on "the floor," where they are employed assembling basic products for local industries and businesses.

Others are placed in a transitional group where the goal is to reach a level of skill to be productive on "the floor." Still others are in need of constant personal attention and show little aptitude or willingness for training.

Charles, who has been at the workshop for 13 years, was in the last group. "He never showed any expression; he was glass-eyed," Utt said.

"I usually say hello to everybody, and I usually get a response," said Julie Hayes, who is also approaching 10 years at Northwestern. "Charles never responded. We thought that was about it for him."

So dislocating was Charles' take to facilitated communication, so dramatic were his missives on the computer screen, that both Utt and Hayes said their outlook and approach to their jobs have undergone drastic transformation.

"I'll never again think that they don't know what's going on," Hayes said. "I will never assume that these people don't have potential."

Charles has since moved to the transitional level, working on exercises designed to strengthen his hands, which, in turn, should improve his control at the keyboard and reduce the facilitator's manual support.

As he progresses, the technique calls for the facilitator to move from hand to wrist to elbows to a finger on the shoulder for emotional support.

"Charles' typing is not clean, there are extra letters in most every word, but it is decipherable and it is improving," Utt said.

Muscle fatigue is a factor as are the neurological handicaps Charles must struggle with, but he persists.

"He feels good about himself now," Hayes said. "He always wants to prove he can do this."

Utt and Hayes aren't guessing when they assess Charles' frame of mind - he's telling them how he feels.

"Imagine knowing what you want to say, but not being able to say it for 36 years," Hayes said. "What's amazing is that he holds no grudge."

Of equal astonishment to Utt and Hayes, but what feeds the skeptics' fire, is that Charles doesn't look at the keyboard or the screen when he types. He has never been taught typing, much less reading or spelling. Yet he can.

Hunt said it is not an uncommon situation in facilitated communication, but as the individual progresses, he is encouraged to look at what he's writing.

When asked by a reporter why he doesn't look, Charles responded: "I hope you understand, I just don't know."

And according to Charles, he learned to spell by watching "Wheel of Fortune."

Not as striking, but just as apparent is the change in Charles' demeanor. He has brightened noticeably, said Lynne Van Evera, his supervisor on the transitional unit. He has also gained the respect of his peers, she said. "They treat him as a person and not just a lump of clay."

Utt and Hayes are at a loss to explain what has unfolded since Charles' first day at the keyboard on March 31, and what several others like Charles have accomplished at Northwestern with facilitated communication.

It still leaves them flush with amazement and even, in Utt's case, a little shaken. "It's changing lives so much it's scary," she said. "But until something changes, I'm a true believer."

'I Love You'

There is no room for doubt in the Hale household. Joy and hope occupy all the available space - flowing from Jane Hale's eyes; spreading with every smile from Martel Hale.

Each word from Charles on the typewriter in the dining room is a sort of deliverance from 36 years of silence. For the first time, the Hales are getting to know their only child - his ambitions, his desires, his needs, his frustrations.

"When he first broke through," Jane said, "it was: 'I love you, I love you,' and then: 'Why do you treat me like a baby?'"

Charles knows facts and dates about himself and his family: where they've lived; who his relatives are.

We had no idea he was absorbing everything," Martel said, adding that the emotional highs that have accompanied Charles' revelations have been dizzying.

Things have settled just a bit, he said, and the focus is now to let Charles proceed at his own pace.

Charles says he wants to be an advocate for those like himself, to show that people without speech are intelligent.

The Hales don't know how far Charles can go, whether he'll ever be able to type independently or whether he will always need a facilitator. It doesn't really matter to them. They have their son back, Martel said, as if he had died and come back to life.

Chapter Three

Family History

THE EARLY YEARS

My husband, Martel, and I, accompanied by my father, U.S. Army Captain (Retired) Clifford A. Gray, and my mother, Olive Jennette Thompson Gray, arrived in Fresh Meadows, New York, in the fall of 1955. Martel, a Special Agent with the FBI, had just been transferred to the New York Office in Manhattan. We were to remain in Fresh Meadows, an apartment complex located on Long Island, 13 miles from Manhattan, until 1979, a year after Martel's retirement from the Bureau.

Martel's father and mother, Robert Earl Hale and Abigail Wallace Hale, as well as my father, were Kentuckians. I first met Martel in Bowling Green, Kentucky, in 1946, when he had just been discharged from the Army Air Corps. He had come back to complete his undergraduate work at Western Kentucky State Teachers College, now known as Western Kentucky University, where I had been a student but was then working as Secretary to the Registrar of the college.

Martel and I were married in 1952, the year before he graduated from the University of Kentucky, College of Law. We were living in Owensboro, Kentucky, in 1954, when Martel joined the FBI and was sent to Pittsburgh, Pennsylvania, where we resided for one year before being transferred to New York City. Our son, Charles, was born there on January 2, 1957.

My husband has one sister, Elizabeth Hale Dawson, and one brother, Robert Maurice Hale, residing in Endicott, New York, and Owensboro, Kentucky, respectively. I am an only child. Before Martel and I were married, we had agreed to take my aging parents with us whenever we moved away from Bowling Green. My father was then in failing health, being in pain much of the time with arthritis of the spine. I could not bring myself to leave my parents. How many people find such a husband, particularly in today's "me" oriented world? In the many years to follow, Martel never wavered in this commitment to me and I will always be grateful. When Charles heard me say that I was going to be writing about our life in New York, he asked that his following comments be included:

"Please, may I tell the story of you and Daddy's love for each other and the love in our family, before we came here, when you and Daddy looked after grandma and grandfather. You two were absolutely wonderful and so unselfish as to keep them both at home, until the end, and also care for me. I have always been proud of you for that and think everyone else should know just what you have lived through. We are so selfish in today's world that we have practically forgotten the real purpose of life. It is to love one another and not always think of ourselves. Thank you for all of your loving care for these many years. You are two remarkable people, and I love you more than life.

I would like to say that I remember mother and daddy lifting grandma and taking her back and forth to the bed many times a day. I remember that mother always fed her first, me second, and daddy third, and then she ate last. She had to clean her up, as she was incontinent, and we ordered diapers, enough to start our own drugstore, and the Wishnia family brought them over almost every night. Before grandma got sick, I can remember grandfather being taken to the hospital for the last time. Mother went over to the hospital every day and night and father stayed at home with grandma and me, until we received word for grandma to come over as he was not expected to live. She went over and I remember both of them coming home and crying. Then mother called Geraldine Roper's mother to come and stay with grandma while the three of us came to Winchester, Virginia, to bury grandfather. Grandma was too worn out to travel. Daddy never complained about the time mother spent caring for the three of us all those years. He is a very special man and I love him dearly."

At the time of Charles' birth, there were several possibilities which could have contributed to his neurological impairment. They are as follow: There could have been a cut off in oxygen during his birth; the delivery was difficult and the doctor mentioned to my husband the possibility that a cesarean section would have to be performed; there was an excessive amount of amniotic fluid, a condition known as hydramnios, during the pregnancy; and, finally, a few hours after birth Charles was placed in isolation with a high fever and remained there for two days. Because of this development, a local pediatrician was called in to examine Charles before we left the hospital. We were told that he could find nothing wrong with our baby.

Any one or a combination of several of the above possibilities might have caused Charles' problems; but, of course, too many years have now passed for us to be certain of the exact cause.

Charles

Charles was definitely a late developer. He sat alone at the age of nine months; he began to walk at the age of eighteen months; and, of course, he is still totally without expressive speech. He never reached out to hold his bottle and never responded to toys. By the age of two and a half years, when we again expressed our concern that something must be wrong with Charles, we were told not to think such things. When Charles was still not talking at the age of three and a half years, we were told that it was still a time to observe. When he was four years and two months old, he began to have akinetic, drop attack seizures, in which he would drop to the floor. He did not appear to lose consciousness as he was up right away; however, there was always the danger of serious injury if he had hit his head in the fall. It was suggested to us that it might be best for him to wear a helmet; we chose not to do so, fearing that such an apparatus would only cause him to be more agitated, and we watched him very carefully instead. We were referred to Long Island Jewish Hospital for an evaluation. The result of Charles' neurological evaluation was as follows: "brain injury with mental retardation due to the injury."

We asked what we could do to help Charles. We were told that there was nothing that could be done to help him and were left entirely on our own to find a support group or whatever services might be available. Two days after this devastating diagnosis, Martel had to leave for the Army Language School in Monterey, California. He would be gone for the next nine months before returning home. Without the love and support of my parents, particularly my mother, I do not know how I would have survived. My mother and I were almost afraid to sleep, fearing that Charles might get out of bed and fall due to his seizures which occurred many times a day.

The long months passed and Martel came home. There were weeks of trying to find the right medication and dosage to control Charles' seizures. We went for second and third opinions concerning the diagnosis including The Kennedy Child Study Center in Manhattan. The diagnosis was always the same. We will never know how an early diagnosis of "autism" might have helped Charles' progress.

After much trial and error with medications, Charles was put on mysoline, an anti-covulscent, which controlled his seizures. Many years later after his breakthrough on facilitated communication, Charles requested that he be taken off this medication as he thought his painful gums might be one of the side effects. Charles' neurologist, Dr. Katherine Gustin, in Winchester, Virginia, slowly decreased his medication. He is now off mysoline and seizure-free. We are grateful to Dr. Gustin for helping us in this way.

By the time Charles was six years old, we had found a volunteer rehabilitation center in the south Bronx. This Saturday program, conducted by a compassionate, dedicated Dr. Jack Gootzeit, later became The Institute of Applied Human Dynamics. In 1965, when Charles was eight years old, he was accepted into The Association for the Help of Retarded Children's school program for the trainable mentally retarded in Queens. For the next fourteen years, until we moved to Winchester, Virginia, this volunteer parent organization provided a lifeline, five-day-a-week service to Charles. We remain indebted for both of the above mentioned services.

SHATTERED DREAMS

It was a May day in 1961 when our dreams for our little boy were shattered. It seemed as though we were two other people and all of this overwhelming sadness which we felt could not be happening to us. "Brain injured with mental retardation due to the injury." What a life sentence for our precious little boy who looked so perfect to us, yet in some strange way which we could not explain seemed so different in so many ways. We then knew what we had wondered about for so long, but would not allow ourselves to believe - Charles was handicapped! Didn't the doctor lead us to believe that everything was going to be all right and that our fears over the years were unwarranted? This empty, completely drained feeling could not be happening to us, but it was.

As my husband and I left Long Island Jewish Hospital, like two zombies leading an angel who had somehow become even more precious to us, we thought of all the ways our lives had changed in just a matter of minutes. As Martel turned onto the lane leading to our apartment, he had to stop the car before we were to reach our building as somehow he suddenly felt that he could not continue to drive and needed to pull over. I remember him leaning his head on the steering wheel and sobbing. He quickly pulled himself together and apologized for his emotional outburst, saying that there were so many things that he wanted to teach Charles. For a few short minutes, it seemed that we had just lost our little four-year-old boy and a part of ourselves forever.

Nothing is more precious to a parent than his/her child; in fact, when something bad happens to that child, most parents would far rather it had happened to themselves. But life is not that way and we have to learn to accept the bad with the good. Most of us do, but it takes awhile. We never seem to get over the heartache and worry, but we somehow learn to cope.

When Martel had to leave for California, only two days after learning about the condition of our son, the timing for even a temporary separation could not have been worse! I still remember the car drawing away from the curb with a bunch of wet socks drying on the back seat, a small testament to the turmoil in our lives at the moment. We were in shock and the mundane, trivial importance of washing socks and getting things in order for an extended trip didn't seem to fall into place. Isn't it strange what we seem to remember over the years -- wet socks!

Our lives have improved. Our beloved son is less disabled than we had been led to believe. With his relatively newfound ability to communicate via facilitated communication, Charles is far more hopeful about his future and so are we. At least now he can tell us of his needs and desires. We hope to give the reader a bird's eye view of what it is like to be verbally disabled and thus open the lines of communication and understanding.

Charles

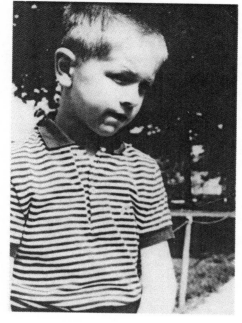

HE'S HYPERACTIVE, YOU SAY?

By the time Charles' seizures were under control with the anti-convulsant, mysoline, at the age of eight, he was admitted to his first Association for the Help of Retarded Children (A.H.R.C.) school program in Queens, New York. This was not a Board of Education program, but was conducted by the educational staff of the A.H.R.C.

Charles entered this program for the trainable mentally retarded with a bang--a quick kick to the shin of his teacher, a kind and experienced man named Stanley Prescott, from the Island of Barbados, who quickly encouraged me to believe that Charles' behavior would improve and not to worry. Fortunately, Mr. Prescott's prediction came true.

Further examples of Charles' frustration and hyperactivity, up until about the time he entered puberty, were very infrequent episodes of uncontrollable screaming at the most inappropriate times. On one particular occasion, Charles and his father were walking down the streets of Manhattan when, suddenly and without provocation, Charles came forth with a loud, guttural scream which lasted for several minutes. Daddy, who ordinarily did not push the panic button as quickly as I, admitted to me that he was greatly perturbed, to say the least, as the thought occurred to him that he just might be accused of extreme child abuse!

On another occasion, when Charles was 12 years old, we had come to Winchester, Virginia, to bury my father. On the trip down, Charles didn't sleep a wink and proceeded to emit a bellowing scream periodically throughout the night. Needless to say Martel and I didn't rest at all that night, and I rather doubt that the other occupants of the motel did either. Many years later, when Charles could finally express himself through facilitated communication, he told me that he was extremely upset by his grandfather's death and his inability to relate his feelings and comfort us. When I look back now, realizing how aware Charles was of any and all happenings in our lives and his inability to let us know, I marvel that he has come as far emotionally as he has. The above mentioned behavior patterns seemed only to occur when Charles was out of his routine and apparently unable to cope.

How about going to an Association for the Help of Retarded Children (A.H.R.C.) meeting one evening only to return home to a state of uproar with the police running up and down the street looking for your young son who, upon seeing that his baby sitter grandmother had inadvertently failed to lock the front door, had decided to go looking for The Good Humor Man? This delectable temptation was ordinarily found outside the local branch of Bloomingdale's three blocks away from our apartment in Fresh Meadows, New York. By the time Martel and I returned home from our meeting, the neighbors were out in every disarray ranging from going out in a police car clad only in a coat over one's slip to darling grandma, engulfed in blankets, sitting on a chair which had been provided for her on the front lawn. We no sooner had time to panic when in comes Charles as pleased as punch, having been rescued from his adventure at his favorite eatery at the side of Bloomingdale's. We had good neighbors who lost no time in taking action.

Charles and his father have always gone grocery shopping together. One afternoon the two of them went out together on this customary tour of a local grocery store in Fresh Meadows when, upon getting ready to leave the store, Martel noticed that his little "Mouse" was not following behind him as was his habit. Upon seeing his predicament, Daddy quickly made a survey of the entire store, ruminating about how he was to proceed from there if he failed to find Charles and what he was going to tell Mother about the loss of her darling son when, out of nowhere, appears his son wearing a mischievous smile. Apparently, another trip to Bloomingdale's and safely back without mishap. Not the greatest thing for one's blood pressure.

The above episodes occurred when Charles was just entering his teens and the third, and hopefully the last, excursion away from the safety of family and friends took place when Charles was about the age of twenty-two. We were visiting our good friends, Marthe and Arnold Ragano, on Long Island, when Charles, who apparently was not momentarily receiving enough attention, decided to make a jaunt to a nearby drugstore, having crossed a very busy thoroughfare and almost succeeding in giving everyone concerned a heart attack! Again, the police were out and made yet another successful capture, much to the relief of all concerned. Many years later, after his breakthrough on facilitated communication, I asked Charles how he managed to escape being hit by a car while gallivanting through such heavy traffic. He nonchalantly replied, "Why, Mother, don't you know that I have always known the 'stop' and 'go' signals?"

Fortunately, Charles no longer displays any desire to go out on his own, much to the relief of his aging parents. He is now 41 years old and the maturation process has seemingly taken place along with the subsiding of the hyperactivity of his youth. Never give up hope. You, too, may be pleasantly surprised.

Chapter Four

Breakthrough

CHARLES BECOMES VERBAL

In the fall of 1979, Martel, Charles and I moved to the city of Winchester, Virginia, located in the beautiful Shenandoah Valley. Fortunately, several weeks thereafter, Charles was able to enter a five-day-a-week program at the Northwestern Workshop here in Winchester. This facility provides both in-facility and community based employment opportunities for adults with disabilities, with the goal being to help individuals find employment of their choice.

Charles, who was among the most disabled, non-productive consumers at the workshop, was believed to be exactly what his original evaluation indicated, "severely or profoundly mentally retarded"; that is, until March 31, 1993, when Susan Utt, a teacher working at the workshop and being assisted by Julie

Hayes, was amazed to see Charles' responses at the keyboard of a computer through the use of facilitated communication. Speaking through the use of this communication technique, with Susan as the facilitator or receiver, Charles' life changed forever! He is no longer silent! His name came through clearly and he was also able to answer other questions correctly. Several days later, to the elation of his parents who were called over to the Workshop to observe this phenomenon, he was still answering questions; and, despite the extra letters coming across the keyboard, the staff diligently made every effort to decipher the messages which were coming through.

Beginning with isolated words and short sentences, Charles began to speak via his right index finger on a computer with his supervisor, Lynne Van Evera, and with me at home on the electric typewriter. Within three or four months, Charles was amazing us with his lengthy and articulate dissertations!

Charles, who is apraxic/dyspraxic ("dyspraxia" being a medical term for difficulty in planning and carrying out complex movements) with the 'A" referring to the absence of something as in his total inability to speak, does not type independently; however the consistency of style, personality, loving attitude and intellect has been validation enough for his several facilitators to date. A person with dyspraxia may have a poor understanding of the messages which the senses convey and difficulty in relating those messages to actions. For example, if Charles is asked to walk across the room, he is not always able to respond to the command; if he is asked to point to a certain part of his body, he may not be able to find that body part and respond to the command. Even though he knows that part of his body very well, he cannot always find it and respond to the command. Due to his movement disorder, Charles would most likely never be able to use the "signing" used by the hearing impaired; however, he does clasp his hands and elevate them to sign "yes." His signal for "no" is to point to his nose; even this is often difficult for him to do upon command. These abilities may vary from day to day. Charles is now more productive in the tasks which his disability does not prevent him from completing. He is also more attentive, by making eye contact and interacting with his co-workers and is now considered to be "autistic." Throughout the book, Charles will be giving examples of his motor planning and sensory integration problems. The terms "apraxia" and "dyspraxia" are often used interchangeably. Most often Charles seems to prefer to use "apraxia" to describe his disability.

Since his breakthrough, Charles has told me that he even remembers being evaluated as a young child in New York City and not having the heart nor the desire to cooperate on tests because he knew that the end result would always be the same, "mentally retarded." Being so neurologically impaired, he holds no animosity toward his evaluators, saying, "How could they have known what was on my mind?" He remembers wanting to cry out and tell them that he was hearing what they were saying about him and that their diagnoses were incorrect!

Mary Jane and Martel

About nine months after Charles' breakthrough, I was invited to speak before a group of Christian Women United at the First Presbyterian Church where I am a member. The following message from Charles is an excerpt from that talk: "I now feel better about myself in every way and I will try my very best to deserve all of the wonderful thoughts and prayers that have come my way. I will try all of my life to keep an uplifted attitude and to remember how much I was loved by you and Daddy and let that serve as an inspiration to try to help others as best I can.

Martel, Jane and Charles

I have so much love for others and I sometimes think that is the reason I was born handicapped, just to let others know that they must live their lives with an uplifted spirit in order that it was not in vain for them to have been born in the first place."

THE LEARNING PROCESS

It is now over five years since Charles' breakthrough on facilitated communication. In some respects I am still "on cloud nine" and in all respects my husband and I are still overjoyed as we continue to hear our son's voice. In retrospect, some very funny things happened to me when Charles and I first began to communicate via FC, and I would like to take the reader back in time to the first few days immediately following Charles' first words on the computer at the Northwestern Workshop here in Winchester.

Remember that Charles began to type only isolated words in response to questions such as "What is your name?" and "Where do you live?" and the basic "Yes" and "No" responses. Both at the workshop and here at home, we were feeling our way in finding out just how cognitive Charles was. With all of the extra letters which came across on the screen, I remember seeing Charles' response to that first question, "What is your name?" It came through loud and clear and, regardless of the flack which was to follow, Susan Utt, Julie Hayes and I knew that we had a "breakthrough." At the age of 36, Charles had joined "the real world." At long last he was freed from his verbal imprisonment.

When Charles was still in the single word or sentence response stage, one evening I asked him if he knew in what language he was speaking. He immediately got up from the typewriter and went into the bedroom and lay down upon the bed. Thinking that perhaps I had insulted his intelligence, I followed him and said, "Charles, I hope I didn't upset you by asking that question." He went back to the typewriter in the other room and, refreshing my mind about a recent conversation which we had had, he exasperatingly, said, "Mother, I just finished telling you the names of everyone buried in our cemetery plot and now you ask me in what language I am speaking!" I believe that was just about the end of my deprecatory questions, at least to that extent! At the time I didn't know much about sensory overloads, but perhaps I had just given Charles one with that last question.

Day by day, and even to date, the learning process continues as we slowly really get to know our son. Upon receiving my first letter from Dr. Douglas Biklen, Director of the Facilitated Communication Institute, in Syracuse, New York, I was rather surprised to learn that Charles was not the only genius, philosopher or Poet Laureate in the world. (I can assure you that is just what it appeared to be after 36 years without hearing his voice!) When my family and I attended our first Facilitated Communication Conference in Syracuse, in 1994, we came to the conclusion that every developmentally disabled person in attendance was exceptional. Freed from their verbal imprisonment through the use of facilitated communication, we were able to see their many faceted individualities, as the intelligent, courageous people they are, possessing a full spectrum of feelings, needs, talents and potential often seen through their educational agenda, writings, art work and poetry.

Chapter Five

Charles and Facilitated Communication

FACILITATED COMMUNICATION (a.k.a. FC) AND FADING WITH CHARLES

Throughout the pages of this book, Charles' use of facilitated communication will be seen with several facilitators. There will be examples of his typing with me as early as four months after his breakthrough on facilitated communication with Susan Utt at the Northwestern Workshop here in Winchester; examples of some of Charles' conversations with Nancy Bagatell, his occupational therapist from Shenandoah University, who is now working toward her doctorate at UCLA; and also with Steve Beck, formerly Charles' In-home instructor from Grafton School.

Some of Charles' first communications with me show much more accuracy as to extra letters being brought in during his typing because, in my anxiety to get good copy to save, I have had a tendency to give his hand more support than is conducive to promoting his future independence on the typewriter. In our daily conversations, when saving the communications is not important to me, less support may have been given, with my supporting hand being moved back to Charles' wrist. This progression of the facilitator, moving from hand, to wrist, to mid-arm and, finally, to a hand on the shoulder for support, is called "fading."

Charles often asked Nancy and Steve to give him more support, explaining that, with his neurological impairment, it is difficult and often even painful for him to look at the keyboard as he types. He doubts that he will ever be independent because of his apraxia; however, he does say that, when we do not believe him to be looking at the keyboard, he is able to see through his peripheral vision.

Charles further explains that his whole sensory perception is much more acute than the norm, often even to the point of pain, with extremely amplified sounds and the seeing of lights during times of stress. This does not seem to be unusual in the world of autism. Often, when Charles is out of his routine environment, or when he is facing a new challenge, we note that this stressful experience, which he refers to as an "overload," must be taking place because he has a squinting, pained expression on his face. According to Leo Kanner, who identified the neurological impairment known as "autism", some 50 years ago, "Sameness" and "Aloneness" seem to be the most identifying characteristics. An example of "sameness" might be seen when an autistic individual is out of his/her normal daily routine, the comfort zone so to speak. I expect the term "aloneness" refers to the autistic person's withdrawal from others at times of frustration, stress and inability to cope. I know that Charles has often expressed his need for inclusion, but has also shown a need to be alone quite often if only for short intervals.

CHARLES EXPLAINS
HIS MOVEMENT DISORDER

"I think my movement disorder is most apparent in the fact that I am unable to respond to someone or something, when my intelligence would tell me to respond in an appropriate manner. For instance, when I should be smiling, sometimes I know that I am not smiling but may be even frowning. This causes me a great deal of pain and makes me look as though I am not comprehending when, in fact, I am crying to respond in an appropriate manner. This also occurs when I am unable to get up and bring something on command. I recognize the object, but I still can not bring it back and appear to be unable to understand the command. This causes me to look as though I am retarded rather than autistic. It is all very complicated, and I hope people will begin to understand that appearances do not always indicate how a person thinks and responses do not show our abilities.

My inability to wave to my parents as a young child was a result of the brain not being able to respond to my desire to that part of my body which would enable me to wave. I know that it is difficult for anyone to understand unless he has the problem himself. If people could give us a chance in life to prove ourselves, many people would be happier and feel a part of society and not just misfits. Another example of this problem is when I am unable to go to the bathroom as a man and not a woman. For example, in order for me to urinate, I must sit down and this causes one to feel that I am mentally retarded. I feel terrible about this, but can not seem to change my way of going to the bathroom. I was not toilet trained until late and I feel that this disturbance in my motor perception kept me from being trained earlier. I received my mother's message but could not respond. This distressed me very much and probably caused my delay in responding altogether. I hope parents will begin to understand that we will be trained as soon as our bodies allow us to respond appropriately. This will cause far less hassle in growing up.

I remember my friend, Nancy Bagatell, telling my mother that I did not know the parts of my body in space. This is absolutely true as I often cannot find my nose on my face or know where my shirttail is when my mother asks me to pull it up when I go to the bathroom. I just do not seem to get the command to respond and find my shirttail to keep it from getting wet. I know where it is, but I cannot seem to find it upon command. This is very frustrating as you can imagine. It causes me to appear mentally retarded when I feel that I am actually quite intelligent. Another thing that is frustrating is when I am unable to ask for something and must always resort to the typewriter or word processor to make the request.

I hope that I have not been too graphic in explaining all of the above but I want to help both parents and professionals to understand people with movement disturbances and apraxia better. Can you understand now why there are so many behavior problems with this population? We are so mentally disturbed most of the time that it is a wonder we can function at all. I believe I function better all of the time because of my parents' love and because of all those people trying to help me get through this life with a little dignity and happiness. I love them all for all of their loving care and concern. Please try to understand and be patient with us. We are trying to be good citizens and good people."

CHARLES CONVERSING, VIA FC, WITH HIS OCCUPATIONAL THERAPIST, NANCY BAGATELL, IN DECEMBER, 1997. IN A QUESTION AND ANSWER SESSION, NANCY ASKS CHARLES ABOUT HIS MOVEMENT DIFFERENCE - The following was for a study:

N. How are you today?
C. I plan to go to the Syracuse.
N. For the Conference?
C. Yes.
N. Did you have a nice Thanksgiving?
C. O.K. How about you?
N. Good.
N. When do you feel like you get stuck the most
C. I get stuck plenty. when my body is doing different things from my mind.
N. Do you feel like you get stuck in certain positions?
C. Yes, Too many times I get stuck in the motion.
N. Do you have more trouble starting or stopping a motion?
C. Starting.
N. Do you ever have trouble switching a motion?
C. Yes. That is very hard for me.
N. Do you get stuck more often when performing tasks you are unfamiliar with?
C. Yes
N. Why?
C. I'm not looking at the keyboard because my eyes bother me. Because I don't know the motion.
N. What environmental factors play a part in your movement difference?
C. The lights, the sound, the people.
N. Does temperature affect you?

34

C. You know, I never thought about that.

N. **Are there some tasks you perform in which you never experience movement difference?**

C. I don't think so.

N. **Even those you perform everyday?**

C. Yes.

N. **Do you experience movement differences more at home or at the workshop?**

C. More at home since things change so much.

N. **What is your awareness in the times when you get stuck in a movement?**

C. I am very aware of being stuck. I feel stupid.

N. **What strategies do you use when you are stuck to resume movement?**

C. I try to think about the movement and put my energy to letting my body relax.

N. **Do you feel stress when you are stuck?**

C. Yes. It feels like I am doing a marathon just to move.

N. **What advice would you give someone who prompts you to move. When should the person assume you are stuck?**

C. When I look like I'm not moving.

N. **What should someone do?**

C. Tell me and touch my hand.

N. **What do you want people to understand about movement difference?**

C. That it is a problem that most people don't understand. That I like to tell people that people with movement differences are not stupid. That you need patience and understanding.

N. **If you had one wish, what would it be?**

C. That I could talk.

N. **Charles, is there anything else you would like to talk about related to the study?**

C. Yes, I hope that this has been helpful. I liked the kids that came to the workshop. (Charles is speaking with regard to a study which Nancy and her students from Shenandoah University conducted with Charles at the Northwestern Workshop.)

This conversation took place in August 1996 between Charles and Steve Beck (with Steve Beck acting as facilitator):

i think i could use more support
justhb righgt now i feel more comfortabkle
How did the exercises make you feel?
i feel like the exercises fior my hands and concentration are very good for me to prqactice
Do you think they help you with typing and other parts of your life?
i know that there ae somethungs that i swill pronbably never be able to do on my own like typing for one
Are you still hopeful that you will be able to type independently someday?
i am always hopeful but i know that i will have limitations that i will not ovesdrcome
But haven't we seen some progress?
yes but you must understandf how hard it is to be ab le tgo recognize all of the ways you need to changve but to not be abler to cause your vbody to do so
I noticed that it is particularly difficult for you to perform tasks on command. Why is this?
i can not really explain it any better than yto sesy tjhat i hear the command but there jis a complete inability for my body to respio0n nd to the request physicslly
That must be very hard to have to cope with while it is happening. You appear frustrated; is that the right word?
yes but is is mre than just emotinally frustrating it is very opainful to feel the body not resonding to my brain command

FACILITATED COMMUNICATION/
CIVIL RIGHTS

Under the U.S. Constitution, the first amendment provides the right of freedom of speech. Civil rights are now being denied to the most vulnerable of our citizens, when they are called upon, in many instances, to prove that they are speaking and that, in every instance, what they are saying is valid. Do we require this of anyone else? I am speaking of those of our citizens who have no expressive speech through the use of their own voice. In this book we are primarily looking at the autistic population, many of whom are totally apraxic and without the use of facilitated communication would still be imprisoned within their own bodies. Their nervous systems have developed differently than the norm. They normally do not respond to tests in the same way that most people do. This is not because they are not cognitive or because they would not want to be cooperative when they are called upon to prove themselves. Most assuredly, they are crying out to us for our understanding. They may be responding to a stimulus in the only way that they are able; and, because their response is not what "we" expect of them, they are too often regarded as questionable. It is often difficult to give validity to individuals who are speaking through a facilitator and who do not type independently; however, some of the nonverbal have become independent in their typing and, consequently, are typing on their own. This accomplishment may not validate every individual who is using the technique, but does it not validate facilitated communication itself? How could anyone think that it is not a viable tool for the nonverbal or the speech impaired?

In the words of Charles Hale, Jr.: "i feel tyhat fc is an inerfficient and insufficient form of communication but it is the blessing that has opened the world to me.

i know the truth isv that most people are skeptical of fc and den7y any valicdatio0ns but there is no disputinvgg the fact tyhat many non verbal autistic people have very intelligent and creative minds capsableb of understanding a language which remsains physically unusable until we discovfrr a way to express

37

this understanding like the use of facilitated support to type or use a communication board.

i mean tthast i know tyhat fc does bnot permit me to communi9cate as quickly as sppoken conversation and i can not shyow my feelings and emotrions through the dsounds of words n this iesb frustrating because i still hav4e these ffeelings but have no reqal eway to express them.

preoiple think ythat autistic individuals wswant to withdraw form the rest of society but this is unytrue

the frustratuioion of understanding a language but nkiot neing able to usud n use itcause us to withdraw fc allows us to emerge from ou5r cloedsed worlfd tioo live in thye rewal world.

i hope thyat peop;le will opew n thseir minds and hearts to people who can not speak out to be heard we are full of love and the desire to feel good about ourselves like anyoneb else because facilitated communication is iour hope we believe in it

please try to understand this our voice."

ATTENDING THE CONFERENCE

ON FACILITATED COMMUNICATION
SYRACUSE, NEW YORK

When Martel, Charles and I attended the 1994, 1996 and 1998 Conferences on Facilitated Communication, sponsored by Syracuse University, under the direction of Dr. Douglas Biklen, it was most rewarding for our family. We found all three conferences to be very informative and inspiring. During the 1994 conference, just a year after Charles' breakthrough, we met Nancy Bagatell, an occupational therapist who was planning to move to Winchester. Nancy expressed a desire to work with Charles and, after moving here, she worked with him for a period of three years. Nancy, who was on the staff of Shenandoah University, located in Winchester, invited Charles to speak with her occupational therapist students on several occasions with Nancy as the facilitator. Martel, Charles and I have joined an autism parent support group which was organized by Nancy and currently meets once a month.

At the 1994 conference, Charles spent half of the time fighting his allergy and, no doubt, sensory overloads brought on by too many new experiences, sights and sounds.

In 1996, it was another story. He was able to attend more workshops and, in addition to communicating with his peers, even do facilitated communication with a total stranger. His friend, Nancy, acted as Charles' facilitator during a workshop at which several nonverbal individuals had an opportunity to speak with one another through the technique of facilitated communication. It was a thrilling experience for our family and, because of this, Charles is now communicating with several new friends by letter and e-mail. They are all remarkably proud, intelligent young men who have not given up on life by any means; in fact, during his initial conversation with two of them, Charles asked, "How do I join the work force and how do I find a girlfriend"? Certainly an indication of his desire to join the main stream! Through their use of facilitated communication, they are showing us examples of true courage and hope for the future which, in spite of their struggle with autism, has never died. Their pain and isolation seem to have only strengthened their determination to show the world how much love and talent they have to offer. The real tragedy would have been for us to have not had the opportunity to hear their voices via facilitated communication.

Further on in the book, the reader will hear Charles speaking about one of his new friends, Tom Page, with whom he feels a close affinity in both attitude and disability, and read the personal account of another breakthrough on facilitated communication as told by Charles' friend, Lincoln Grigsby, and Lincoln's mother, Joan Mariah. Tom and Charles are the same age and Lincoln, four years younger.

Will Turnbull and Charles (right)

During the 1998 conference, Charles continued to be able to attend all of the workshops with his father and me, with no apparent sensory overloads. After a workshop, we would often go up to our room and Charles would give account of what he had learned while attending. At the above conference we also met Janna Woods who is currently an administrator on Lincoln's residential staff in Fairfax, California. Charles was able to converse with Janna as she acted as his facilitator. One morning we met Will Turnbull and his mother, Ellie, for breakfast at the Sheraton. Twenty-three year old Will is now a college student, a wonderfully talented young man who just happens to be autistic. Jim, Ellie and Will, whom we first met at the 1996 conference, have visited us here in Winchester. Other highlights of the 1998 conference were having the opportunity to speak with Dr. Biklen regarding our book; speaking with Rosemary Crossley and receiving some valuable advice concerning Charles' visual problems; and, also having the opportunity to meet and hear young Sharisa Joy Kochmeister, college student and advocate extraordinarie. It was also especially delightful to meet and become better acquainted with two e-mail friends, in person, for the first time, Judi Barta and Noni Morrison. Noni accompanied her talented daughter, Melinda, with whom I was able to speak via facilitated communication. Judi and her sister, Barbara Axline, were representing their brother, Doug Hahn, who was not in attendance. We enjoyed hearing Rita Rubin speak about her exceptional college student daughter, Sue.

We also enjoyed having an opportunity to visit, at length, with the Page family, Jo, Wally and Tom, and to see Tom's writing exhibits in the Bulletin Board room, meet another e-mail correspondent, Rita Treacy, and her son, Dan, and view his composition, speak with Anoja Rajapatirana and see young Chammi's talents exhibited, and meet the gracious Pat Edwards, Coordinator of the FCNet, as well as visit with other family advocates and professionals in attendance at the conference. We did miss seeing our friends, the Moisuks, Cornelia, Jack and John, Jr., who could not attend the conference because of illness.

When we attended the FCNet Social, Charles seemed to be looking for someone. All of a sudden, he disappeared and was heading down the floor, at a fast pace, having espied his friend, Tom Page. When I finally caught up with Charles, and acted as his facilitator while he visited Tom, he said, "Tom, you are my very best friend in the world as you are the only one who really understands me!" Charles has often told me how much alike the two of them are. What a delight to see them relating to one another.

One of the workshops which we found most interesting was the one on Going to College with Facilitated Communication, at which we had an opportunity to hear Dr. Biklen, Rita Rubin and Sharisa Joy Kochmeister speak. Sharisa Joy was accompanied by her devoted father. This workshop included attention to what kinds of transition issues occurred, the supports that have been helpful and reflections on life in college, including both academic and social experiences. Sue Rubin was unable to attend because of college finals.

Another outstanding workshop which we were able to attend was the Exposure Anxiety: The Problem of Daring to Be. This keynote presentation by renowned author Donna Williams was about experiencing autism and entering the world. Her first book, Nobody Nowhere, became an instant best seller. Today it is a classic in disability autobiographies. Donna Williams is one of the leading analysts of autism on the international scene, speaking from an insider's perspective.

It was also our privilege to hear Eugene Marcus' keynote presentation on Almost Becoming a Person. He spoke about his ongoing journey toward realizing that only he can set his goals and know when he has reached them. The discussion was about drawing a fiery line between being real, which he always had been, and being normal, which he never would be. He spoke about how well meaning professionals needed to make that clear distinction. Mr. Marcus is a man with autism who believes in his own rights and those of others with and without disabilities. He is now an associate of the Facilitated Communication Institute, where he has conducted research on his own means of communication, and lectures frequently on facilitated communication and the rights of people with disabilities. After hearing the speech by this courageous young man, Charles made the following comment: "I hope that I will be able to do that one day."

Due to my ambulatory problem, I was unable to attend the dinner featuring Rosemary Crossley as keynote speaker, but I was able to obtain her Breaking the Silence audio cassette and was grateful to be able to hear her speech. I, personally, feel that her latest book, Speechless, is another absolute "must" for anyone wishing to better understand people with developmental disabilities, as is Dr. Biklen's Communication Unbound, which was published in 1993. Of course, I know that I would be interested in reading anything written by either of these two scholars.

Another workshop which was of particular interest to our family was the one on Vision: A Missing Link Affecting Communication which was conducted by Dr. William Padula. This presentation explored the issues of vision and autism and its relationship to communication. The presenter gave a basic understanding of the anatomy and neurology of vision, covered the vision process and discussed two syndromes involving the visual system that are commonly identified in people experiencing developmental disability. Charles, after hearing Dr. Padula speak about the visual midline shift syndrome, told us that he believed that this syndrome did, indeed, apply to him. We are now in the process of checking out the possibility that a behavioral optometrist might help Charles to solve his focalizing problem and enable him to look directly at the computer or letterboard rather than relying mainly on his peripheral vision. This, of course, should promote his ability to work toward typing independence. After hearing the above lecture, it is our understanding that a jammed focal process interferes with speech and language as well as facilitated communication.

My family and I have always come away from these Facilitated Communication Conferences, in Syracuse, with renewed hope and a feeling that each conference was better than the last.

A further example of Charles' improvement in social graces was the fact that we were able to eat in a Sheraton restaurant, for the first time, without the trauma of Charles' frequent coughing spells which always seemed to be brought on by his feelings of inadequacy in certain social situations, particularly when in the homes of friends or in restaurants where he may be asked to eat. Charles is very aware of his lack of coordination in eating and handling silverware. The very fact that he was able to eat in a restaurant, during the entire conference, rather than having to eat in our room, was a special joy for his father and me. To us, this is just one more example of Charles' gradual entrance into what he often refers to as "the real world."

43

FREEDOM FROM IMPRISONMENT

One of the most disturbing things about discovering that Charles has been misdiagnosed for so many years, and perhaps would have remained imprisoned in silence for the remainder of his life but for the technique of facilitated communication, is the thought that there may be many more people like Charles who are still believed to be cognitively disabled to the point of no return. With the relatively new concept of movement difference/disturbance, in addition to our knowledge of apraxias, either of which might cause the nonverbal person to appear to be severely or profoundly mentally retarded, unless a severely motor impaired person is given the opportunity to use facilitated communication, when he may be unable to use a pointer, eye control method on a computer or other augmentative device, he could possibly remain silent forever. I, personally, know of cases where conscientious parents have not sought to have facilitated communication offered to their verbally disabled child even after learning of the help from which others have benefited from its use. I don't know if their reluctance to try facilitated communication, or even other augmentative possibilities for communication, is because the fear of failure, after experiencing a renewed flicker of hope, is too painful to contemplate in its finality, or if it is because they feel absolutely certain that their child would not be able to benefit from any technique of communication in the first place. I rather suspect that it may be the latter reason.

The controversial aspect of facilitated communication and the very vocal parents or professionals, who may have been falsely accused or the recipients of its misuse, have caused some people to be afraid to try the technique with their loved one. This is unfortunate because I feel that a reasonable person should now be able to see the validation of the technique itself. There are more and more individuals all over the world who are now typing independently, or very close to it, and others whose lives have changed so drastically, after their successful use of the technique, that it seems only logical that their improvement in large part is due to their freedom from imprisonment.

After hearing what Charles has had to say about the pain of his inability to verbally express himself before the introduction of facilitated communication into his life, I hope that both parents and professionals will keep an open mind to using some form of augmentative communication with all verbally disabled people. To allow a nonverbal individual to go through life in so much pain and frustration, once his particular means of communication may have been found, is heartless to say the least. It has not been too many years since many severely impaired with cerebral palsy were believed to be severely or profoundly mentally retarded. Even one lost soul who is needlessly locked away in silence is one too many!

If you are a parent, teacher or care provider for a nonverbal or speech impaired child or adult, please give the individual the benefit of the doubt by offering some form of communication facility. It seems to me that any risk which one may have to take in offering a nonverbal person a means to communicate is far less than the consequence of denying him a better life. So many have been, and perhaps still are, so valiantly, patiently waiting.

ASKING FOR HELP

Charles is still very handicapped in so many ways, but he has taken a big step forward toward allowing us a glimpse of the person he aspires to be. Just recently he asked us to consider seeking psychotherapy for him in order that he may start to overcome his "feelings of inadequacy in social situations." In social situations! Isn't that a big order for an autistic person whose typical behavioral characteristic is supposed to be "aloneness" and "sameness?" I feel that the fact that Charles has recently begun to have so many different people coming into our home to try to help him, in addition to his workshop program, has given him more confidence and made him want to reach out for more experiences in what he calls "the real world." Being verbally isolated for so many years has most assuredly curtailed his overall development, but now he is just beginning to burst forth like a brand new butterfly freed of its cocoon and entering a new world.

We have tried to assure Charles that each one of us has felt his/her own feelings of "inadequacy" many times during the course of his/her life, and that he should hold his head up high and seek to derive all the joys of life which he so richly deserves. Seeing him develop into the warm and loving person he has been allowing us to see, during these past five years since his breakthrough, has inspired those of us who love and work with him daily to strive even harder to see that he reaches his full potential, whatever it may be.

While attending the 1996 Conference on Facilitated Communication, we were fortunate enough to attend Anne Donnellan's keynote address in which she explained the differences which may occur in the development of the human nervous system. I had just finished reading Movement Differences and Diversity in Autism/Mental Retardation, the book she co-authored with Martha Leary (DRI Press, 1995). Upon reading this revolutionizing new era concept with regard to understanding and accommodating persons with communication and behavior challenges, I have begun to better understand Charles' sensory problems and movement differences for the first time. I, personally, feel that the above mentioned book is a "must" reading for every parent or professional trying to understand and help a neurologically impaired individual.

Although Charles, fortunately, is not a behavior problem, by reading the above-mentioned book, I now feel that I have a much better understanding about the reasons for his inability to accomplish so many things that his mental ability seems to indicate that he should be able to do. If doctors evaluating Charles so long ago had understood the concept of movement differences, he may have received a diagnosis of autism rather than mental retardation and have been able to receive the proper kind of help sooner; but, then again, so many years ago autistic people were not understood and diagnosed as they are today. Once an evaluation goes down on record it is very likely to remain the same particularly in the case of a nonverbal individual who is virtually untestable because of so many overlays. Facilitated Communication, and the resulting realization of Charles' cognition, allowed us to begin to see his degree of comprehension whereas, with the complexity of his apraxia/dyspraxia, routine testing most likely would not. When one finds that the disabled person has a good mind, there is so much more to hope for and to strive to accomplish. With the better understanding of neurological impairment with which professionals seem to be fortified, the future looks brighter for so many.

Chapter Six

Professional Evaluations of Charles

Susan Utt, who was Charles' facilitator at the time of his breakthrough, speaks about Charles:

"Some might say that I helped to open a new world for Charles, but he not only opened my world, he rearranged it in many ways. I had become very comfortable in my teaching at Northwestern Workshop. Each day was fun and different. There was a common thread that wove its way through my teaching day that gave me security and a comfort level. I was content teaching the academic and independent living skills to my students. My teaching experience was good, but it was not remarkable.

I first learned of facilitated communication while watching an evening "magazine" news show. A week later I had dinner with a friend who used facilitated communication in her work. We talked about it, and she showed me some basic techniques. With this limited knowledge, I took my first step into an intriguing world.

The journey with Charles via facilitated communication has touched many emotions and thoughts within me. The absolute thrill that I experienced when we first worked together is what teachers spend years hoping might happen in their classrooms. Everyone was excited and wanted to know more about facilitated communication. As the headline in the newspaper read, Charles was truly a miracle. Then came the questions and doubts. People asked if I were moving his hand - if even in my subconscious. I had received some training in facilitated communication by this point, but I still felt inadequate to answer the accusations. I could not explain how facilitated communication worked, but I knew what I saw in Charles.

Charles has come to life in an entirely new way. Before he was someone that I spoke to, but I did not expect a response from him. I knew who he was, but I truly did not know him. It was a non-dimensional relationship. He was at the Workshop almost everyday, but no one expected him to do any work. Now Charles responds when I say good morning. He smiles and offers his hand as a greeting. I watch him work and be productive. I have learned of his likes and dislikes, his thoughts and opinions. He is a complete person with a many faceted personality. The total person that I know as Charles Hale has always been there. I just did not know it. Through the wall of silence, I had missed this wonderful person.

Facilitated Communication has done much for Charles. The obvious is that he has a means of communicating, but it has done much more than that. He presents himself with more confidence, and those around him see him with new respect. People want to know what he thinks, and his opinion is valued. Where once those around him did almost everything for him, he now shows a new independence. He rides the city bus to work, and he is missed when he is not there.

My facilitation time with Charles is unpredictable. Some days we truly connect and his typing is fluid. Other days he types letters that make no sense, and I become confused. I wish that each session were strong and full of new ideas, but this is not the reality. After all, some days we do not feel like talking, and silence has to be respected. But where once he spent his entire life in silence, he now speaks to the world. After the many years of quiet, he now reminds us that all people are complete people. We just need to take the time and to find the way to listen to each other. Everyone has a gift to share, and Charles has given me more than I could ever have hoped to receive."

Lynne Van Evera, Charles' supervisor at the Northwestern Workshop, had the following to say about Charles' progress:

"I have known Charles since 1983. The changes I have witnessed since facilitated communication came into his life have been remarkable. I can fully understand how skeptics may not believe in facilitated communication and, possibly, only those of us who know him well can see the changes in his quality of life. If nothing else, I now see Charles differently. This is not only that I believe in his superior intelligence because of the positive validations which I have had from him since he began facilitated communication, but also because of the changes that I have witnessed at the Workshop. For example, he can now follow more complicated directions and he does more physical types of work. He is able to show appropriate emotions more readily. He certainly seems to want to take a more active role in his course of life. No longer does he have to sit when he would rather walk nor does he have to accept chocolate when he would rather have vanilla."

The following evaluation was made by Nancy Bagatell, Charles' occupational therapist, formerly on the staff of Shenandoah University, who worked with him on facilitated communication for three years:

"Like many professionals, I first approached facilitated communication with some skepticism. But in an effort to understand current trends in the field of autism, I attended an FC training through the Adriana Foundation. I returned to my workplace and with some trepidation, began to employ the techniques I had just learned. I soon found that the technique was one that appeared viable for many of the individuals with whom I worked. Not only was it viable but very successful. Individuals who had not shown interest in many purposeful activities and demonstrated short attention spans were now sitting for more than 30 minutes at a stretch. I discussed topics as diverse as politics, movies and emotions with these individuals who had been silenced their entire lives. I saw individuals gain rights and be exposed to new opportunities based on their new found ability to express themselves.

That was seven years ago and in those seven years I have learned a lot. Being involved with FC has not always been easy or pleasant. I have learned that change is hard and that new ideas can be frightening to others. I have seen individuals gain a means to communicate only to have that opportunity whisked away. I continue, however, to use FC with individuals who are interested in using it. I continue to learn much each time I facilitate - about communication, processing of information, movement differences, touch and relationships. While the lives of many people with disabilities have changed as a result of FC, so has mine and I am grateful to those individuals who have trusted me enough to allow me to facilitate with them.

I first met Charles in the fall of 1994. I had recently moved across the country and was thrilled to find someone who used facilitated communication! Charles and I had to establish a firm relationship before typing together became a comfortable process. Initially Charles would type for a few minutes and then get up in mid-sentence and leave the room, needing lots of encouragement to return and "finish his thoughts." With time, however, Charles was able to sit and type with me for 30 to 40 minutes without a break. Charles began to initiate conversation, asking me many personal questions and never failing to give me his opinion about a topic. One of our goals was to work toward independence. This has proven to be a difficult process given the significance of his movement problems. Charles has great difficulty initiating movement and lacks steadiness in his movements. The touch provided through FC appears to help Charles organize his movement patterns and slow and steady his hand, thus increasing his accuracy. We have only been able to "fade back" support minimally. Charles expresses increased anxiety with less support and often prefers to type with more support so that he can "get out" what he wants to say since with less support his typing is slow and less accurate. In any case, Charles remains motivated to communicate his thoughts and feelings and hopefully, as we begin to learn more about movement differences in individuals with autism, we will develop new strategies to use to facilitate independence with FC."

Connie and Cecil Clem, Charles' standby guardians, are two of God's greatest blessings. Connie, an administrator at Grafton School, recently sent us the following comments:

"How could I have known that God would give me a second very special brother? For that is what Charles Hale is to me. From the first time we met, I knew Charles was very alert, aware and intelligent. And now I know that he understands that we have a special bond that will last all over lives.

Often Charles' parents will ask me "Is it a burden for you to be Charles' standby guardian?" My answer is always "No, it is a joy." Charles seems to understand all this. As he follows me through my gardens in the summer time, I tell Charles he will always be welcome here. He gives me a look that lets me know he is glad we are friends.

Life leads us down many paths. On one of my journeys I met the Hales. And how fortunate for me. They have given me love, kindness and a better understanding of my life's work, working with people with disabilities.

Since Charles is an only child, his parents have worried about what will happen should he live longer than they. I'm not sure I have all the answers, but I am sure God meant for us to be one family. So Charles will continue to be my brother. I will treat him no differently. If he needs me, I will be there. I am fortunate in that my husband feels the same. And, in return, Charles has already enriched our lives with his smile, his gentleness, his watchful gaze out his front window when he knows we are coming for a visit, and so much more. I wonder how I will ever be able to repay Charles and his family. Everything would never be enough, for I love them and I will forever be grateful for their love to me."

Chapter Seven

A Potpourri of Comments by Charles

A POTPOURRI OF COMMENTS BY CHARLES

TO MOTHER:

"I don't think it is humanly possible for another person to understand the emotional trauma of a person locked into a body that can't speak. I know that I would have not survived at all but for the love of you and Daddy and that I am still mentally disturbed without speech and that is why I am anxious for someone to work with me on my own voice. You are so good to spend so much time in trying to help me."

CHARLES' MOTTO:

Charles' motto, which now hangs on the entrance wall of the Northwestern Workshop here in Winchester, Virginia, is as follows:

"NEVER UNDERESTIMATE HOW MUCH A PERSON CAN DO-OR FEEL- OR KNOW!"
Charles Martel Hale, Jr.

CHARLES ASKING DOCTORS AND EDUCATORS TO BE CAREFUL IN MAKING A DIAGNOSIS:

"I hope that facilitated communication will allow doctors and educators to be very careful when making a diagnosis for an individual. It is very difficult, I know, for anyone to diagnose accurately an individual who is so severely incapacitated that he can not find his mouth on his face or touch his nose upon command. Also, when one is unable to speak at all, a person doing the diagnosing might have the tendency to believe the individual is severely or profoundly retarded. Being nonverbal does not always mean mental retardation.

I am so happy that my family and I are living proof that a family can survive for many years as long as there is love and affection between the members. I hope that others may take inspiration from my miraculous breakthrough and not give up hope. It would seem, at this point, that my own voice is not going to come through; however, I have to remember that only a few months ago I had no means of communication and now I have!"

CHARLES SPEAKS OF HAVING NO MEANS OF COMMUNICATING:

"I think I had no means of communication before facilitated communication, but I did make my needs known by pointing, going and getting objects and by distress signals in the way of behavior abnormalities and stressful sounds and mannerisms from my vocal cords.

I don't know how I lived through it, but I did have my loving family and teachers who were always by my side. I hope others will not have to spend a lifetime in imprisonment because of the miracle of facilitated communication. I hope that teachers and parents will make every effort to bring other nonverbal people through on facilitated communication."

CHARLES EXPLAINING HIS IMPROVEMENT BECAUSE OF FACILITATED COMMUNICATION:

"i believe my greatest improvement since my breakthrough on facilitated communiation has been my ability to do more productive work at the northwestern workshop. i am now able to complete tasks assigned without prompting and without constant lack of attention. my teacher, lynne vanevera and her assistant, leona weatherholtz have been very patient with my efforst and i can see it proving to be beneficial in that i am now able to szee my potential on the workfloor.

probably my greatest improvement at homr jsas been my ability to communicate with my darling parents and this has caused me to be happier than i ever thought possible. my mother's constant attention to me has made it possible for me to commu icate with the world and with my friends and other loved ones. my mmopthrer is the greatest and so are the teachers, susan utt, julie hayes, leona weatherholtz and lynne vanevera at the workshop. i thank god for allowing me to live to see this day. i will be grateful as long as i live for all of the people besides my mother and father who have been by my side."

CHARLES SPEAKS ABOUT TYPING INDEPENDENTLY:

"Let's talk about my desire to be independent on the typewriter.

I think people might like to hear about how I feel about my inability to be independent. It is terribly frustrating to me because I know I could speak much more if I could send messages on my own. Please let us speak often, even though we are not independent, as we are so frustrated at having to wait for someone to be there to type with us. We are so frustrated most of the time when we are unable to speak that we are mentally ill much of the time.

I hope that I can be independent one day but I don't know if I can concentrate to look at the keyboard for each letter as I need to do to select a letter independently. I do not mean the facilitator is steering me, but supporting my hand allows me to type without looking. To be independent I must look for the letters myself. It is not that the facilitator steers me but gives me the support which allows me to reach out. If I did it alone I must look to even get started.

I see through peripheral vision but not well enough to be independent in typing by myself. That requires more concentration and coordination to do it without the support of a facilitator. When I say support I do not mean guidance as I am always doing that with my forefinger."

AFTER SEEING ANOTHER BREAKTHROUGH ON FACILITATED COMMUNICATION ON TV:

"It is another feather in the hat of facilitated communication. I love Dr. Biklen for helping to tell the world that it is working for many people. He should feel very proud of being a true pioneer in the field as well as a fine man and a friend to all of the nonverbal people in the world. I love him so much and I hope we get to go to the conference in May. I hope that we can at least go for one day."

CHARLES EXPRESSES HIS THOUGHTS ABOUT LEARNING:

"I THINKTHE REASDON PEOPLE WANT TO TELL US THAT IT IS IMPOSSIBLE FOR US TO HAVE LEARTNED SO MUXC HON OUR OWN WITHOUT HAVING HAD A FORMAL EDUCATION IS THAT WE ARE HANDICAP4PED AND NOT BELIEVED TO BEALERT AND INTELLIGENT ENOUGH TO HAVE ABSORBED FACTS AND OTHER INFORMATION ON OUR OWN INITIATIVE. WE HAVE BEEN LISTENING AND LEARNING SINCE THE TIME OF OUR BIRTH AND PERHAPS BECAUSE WE HAVE BEEN SO ISOLATED WE HAVE BEEN MORE ABLE TO RETAIN AND CONCENTRATE WHEN PEOPLE THOUGHT THAT WE WERE VEGETA TATING.

I HAVE LEARNED HOW TO ADD AND SUBTRACT ON MY OWN RATHER THAN IN A CLASSROOMBECAUSE I HAVE LISTENED TO PEOPLE TALKING ABOUT MATEMATICS AND HOW THEY ADD ANDSUBTRACT AND I THINK THAT I MAY HAVE A SPECIAL APTITUDE FOR THAT SUBJECT. I THINK I MIGHT HAVE ABSORBED MUCH MORE IN MY TRAINABLE CLASSES THAN ANYONE EVER REALIZED, BECAUSE I REMEMBER VERA PISTEL SHOWING US ON THE BLACKBOARD HOW TO ADD AND SUBTRACTY

AND THEN I ALWAYS LISTENED TO MY PARENTS TALKING ABOUT ADDING AND SUBTRACTING IN OU HOME. YOU MUST REMEMBER THAT WEHAD MANY HOURS TOABSORB FACTS.

I ALSO BELIEVE THAT I LEARNED THE ALPHABET BY WATCHING PROGRAMS LIKE WHEEL OF FORTUNE AND PERHAPS EVEN WAY BACK INMY AHRC PROGRAMS FOR THE TRAINABLE MENTALLY RETARDED I MAY HAVE PICKED UP A LITTLE KNOWLEDGE THAT NO ONE THOUGHT I WAS ABLE TO ABSORB. THEN I ALWAYS LISTENED TO MY PARENTS AND THEIR FRIENDS SPEAKING AND THEY USED GOOD ENGLISH AND THAT HELPEDME TO LEARN.

I BELIEVE THE REASON WE NONVERBAL DISABLED PEOPLE NEVER GAVE UP ON LEARNING IS BECAUSE WE ALWAYS PRAYED THAT ONE DAY WE WOULD FIND AMEANS TO LET PEOPLE KNOW THAT WE ARE INTELLIGENT, AND THEN OUR DILIGENCE WOULD PAY OFF."

SPEAKING OF "HAMLET"

Charles listens to cassette tapes and then evaluates:
"I thought Hamlet was fascinating, but I didn't have the education to appreciate the fact that it is the greatest play written by William Shakespeare. I thought the fact that it is his greatest made it worthwhile for me to hear. I thought the theme written about Denmark was also worth hearing and the fact that it is a myth is also fascinating and makes me want to learn more about Greek mythology. I wish Daddy would tell me more about Greek mythology. I would also like to learn more about William Shakespeare's other works.

I would also like to learn more about why the world turns around and why it is round and not flat and I hope you will get me some science books which might explain this to me."

RICHARD NIXON:

"I thought Richard Nixon was a great historian of the political arena. He continued to work for world peace by going to China and the other countries to negotiate in our behalf and in behalf of all world peace and understanding."

WORKING TOWARD THE G.E.D.:

"I think that I would like to get my high school diploma, because without it I could never go very far in the work force. Lynne said that I would have to work very hard at home and at the workshop in order to prove myself as a candidate for the diploma but she thinks that I have the intelligence to get my diploma on my own if I really apply myself. I hope that you and Daddy will help me to get ready to pass the G.E.D. I heard someone at the workshop speaking about someone getting a diploma by just passing the test. I realize that this will take a lot of work on everyone's part but I do want to try to work toward this if you and Daddy will help me."

CHARLES SPEAKING OF SENSES WITH REGARD TO HIS INFORMAL EDUCATION:

"There are five senses and they are sight, smell, touch, hearing and taste. I believe that when one sense is absent the other senses become more acute and that is why I am able to hear and see so well when I am not very good at touching.

I hope that I have explained how I have been able to achieve as much education, informally, as I have. I have no formal education. I feel that perhaps I am equivalent to some high school students who do not apply themselves. Perhaps that is one reason that uneducated people with good intelligence can do so well through facilitated communication."

CHARLES DESCRIBES SENSORY PERCEPTION:

"I would like very much to help other people who are without speech and autistic or neurologically impaired.

Sometimes I am unable to hear or see things as clearly as I should and when my random behavior begins, I react in a hyperactive manner. When this occurs it is best to ignore my hyperactivity if at all possible; if it is not possible to ignore my behavior, one should try to remain calm until the random behavior passes. I react adversely to reprimands at this time and I believe other neurologically impaired people would be inclined to do the same. In my particular case, I believe that my hyperactive, random behavior comes when I am frustrated by not being able to speak or by frustration by not being able to do something that my intellect should allow me to do. This is where my apraxia shows itself.

I have always had periods of not being able to see or hear clearly at times only; otherwise, my senses of sight and hearing are very acute. I think that lately my sight has failed at times slightly, particularly when I am watching TV., but not acutely. Perhaps I need glasses which, of course, I would never to able to wear."

CHARLES SPEAKS ABOUT AUTISM:

"I think that a person with autism is apart from other people in the world inasmuch as they never get to relate to people as they would wish to because of their nervous system. I know that many times I am anxious to speak with people and to let them know how much I care about them, but my nerves will not permit me to speak with them even if I had a voice. If people could understand this it would make it more comfortable for them to approach autistic people and then, in turn, it would make the autistic people happier to feel a part of society as a whole. When an autistic person is withdrawn from everyone in the room, that doesn't necessarily mean that he wishes to be ignored; in fact, he may be crying out to say , "Notice me and know that I count too!" It is most frustrating to a person, normal or otherwise, to be ignored.

I would like to urge people not to be afraid to approach the handicapped. They are people just like anyone else and are crying out for love. I think that we must all remember that we don't always go out of this world as we come into it and people must all remember that they haven't finished living and don't know in what condition they will be when they leave. Try to be careful not to forget that we are all in this world together and must learn to relate to one another as best we can."

CHARLES DISCUSSES AUTISM AND APRAXIA:

"I believe that my apraxia involves certain messages being sent to the brain and then, in turn, to different parts of my body. I cannot seem to tell my right from my left although I know my right from my left. I cannot seem to find my mouth upon command. I have trouble finding where my nose is when I am asked. I find that my breath will not come when I am asked to blow or when I am asked to take a deep breath. I am unable to draw through a straw. I have trouble sticking out my tongue. I cannot seem to spit the water out when brushing my teeth. I cannot purse my lips when I want to drink out of a bottle.

I don't seem to get the message to wave or to smile when I should be responding to someone or something. My autism seems to be apparent in my random use of my hands and feet. My habit of biting is a symptom of my being nonverbal and is mostly due to frustration. (The biting which Charles refers to is with regard to things and not people!) I think that autistic or neurologically impaired people do not want to look when asked to because the nervous system is too impaired to receive the message. One sometimes feels that all the lights in the world have been turned on and that everyone is yelling at him. If, for example, a question is asked, the receiver receives the question in a very high pitched tone and even sometimes cannot understand the question. To repeat the question sometimes only makes it more painful.

I think that much of the characteristics of autism is a result of not being able to cope with the neurological impairment which autistic people seem to have. I expect the withdrawal of an autistic person into his own world is a result of this impairment. I also believe that an autistic person's inability to cope makes them less able to concentrate and therefore to learn.

I hope that this evaluation by an autistic individual will help other people to understand that we are intelligent even though we may not always appear to be."

THE FOLLOWING COMMENTS BY CHARLES WERE MADE IN AUGUST, 1996, WHEN STEVE BECK, HIS FACILITATOR, ASKED HIM HOW IT FELT TO BE AUTISTIC:

"do you think i know th e great thingh abou8t the world of ajutism just know this one thing i am no exopert on the verdbal eworld

the life of the aiutitic individuakl is nt not undestzndable in the terms of the non autistic person

it feels lonely to just be alivre

i do not ferl tht anyione xcan x

understand how we feel because the exper5ience of overloads does not make a ny sense to those who do not experiebnce them

i believe that each autizstic person is crying out because we have inteligenrt minds thaft can comprehend lan guage but we can never respond to anyone verbally

i belioeve that fc and other forms of commjnmication are he only tools for non verbal people to try to live in thre verbal world

it maskes it very hard to try to speak when you have to be silelmnt and patiently wait to be assisted to speak

i wishg that there were a more efficident way for us to commnicate because this ixs such a trying process to type without having the contr5ol to type independedntly

i think the positive thing abut fc is the fact that swe can commnicate with the verbal world and finally express ourselves as the intelligent people we are

i truly hope that enough people will learn about the need for efficient communication fo5rtms for no nverbal and motion impaired peoplreb that someone will invent something yto help us in the uture

i think this tyrewriter is thnbe best thing b for meb to learn onn because i know thse com,pputers re the only way t6hawst most peopler4 type n ow

i can zsee the words i am typing becauyse the screen shows the words in large p5riont

i can not always feel the letters ogfthe keyboard so i am not6 sure the words are spell;ped correctly"

CHARLES TYPING WITH HIS FACILITATOR, STEVE BECK, IN AUGUST, 1996, AND SPEAKING OF HIS FRIEND, TOM PAGE, AND THEIR SIMILARITIES:

"It was so nice of Tom to write such a kind letter. You and md (mother dear) seem surprised that Tom and I have so many similarities. It is not that interesting to me because I knew we were experiencing the same things when Tom first wrote. I have felt like the objects I am looking at were broken or seen as many individual objects. I do think that I had more vision overloads before I broke through. That was from the frustration I had from not communicating. I know exactly how Tom feels when he says he is between two worlds. I feel like I do not fit in wherever I am. It makes me feel lonely. It helps a lot to know that Tom has felt and is feeling the same things I experience. It makes it less frightening to go through each day when you know that you are not alone in the world. I do not mean that I have been alone physically but emotionally I feel always by myself. I would love to spend time becoming friends with Tom. I have never had anyone who I felt could understand me. Yes I would love to get together with him but I do not know if it is possible for us to do this. I will look forward to writing Tom a letter. I hope I can express my true feelings and emotions. You know that is the hardest thing about FC. If I do not say what I am feeling perfectly it is not ever understood. I want to go to the library. I thought we had a nice time."

"I MIGHT SAY"

"I might say that I am a great man, but that would not be true.

I might say that I know many things, but that would not be true.

I might say that I loved God, but that would be true.

I might say that I love all people, but I love no one more than God.

I might say that I have been unlucky, but I know that is not true;

I have my family and friends who are wonderful to me.

I might say that I wish I could talk, but I know I never can.

I might say that all of this has been unfortunate; but, in fact,

I have found God and always have Him by my side."

CHARLES ASKING GOD FOR HELP:

"While I was imprisoned in silence for so many years, I kept praying to God to help me and to let my darling parents know how much I loved and appreciate them. They took care of me all my life and never gave up on me even though there were times when I was very difficult to deal with. My mother had her parents to look after in their old age and still found time to help a handicapped son without speech and motivation. God kept me uplifted during the hardest times during my life and He never left my side during the entire time of my trials and tribulations. I feel that without Him I would not have survived to tell my story and to try to help others. My parents continue to help me and so does my faith in God."

CHARLES SPEAKS ABOUT HIS DESIRE TO BE A MINISTER:

"I am very anxious to tell people how much I would like to be a minister. I have always wanted to be a minister, but I know that I can never be. I always wanted to tell people how much I love God and would want them to find comfort in his love. Being locked away so many years, I had much time to think about God and how much I loved him and how much he sustained me in my hours of agony at not being able to speak. I believe that the reason people reach out to Him in times of trouble is that they must have a means of coping and no one else in the world can provide the strength which God in his love provides to all of us if we but reach out to Him in prayer.

I think that God is the reason people are able to survive much heartache and overcome great odds in their daily lives. Please put your trust in our Saviour who gave His all to us on the Cross. Our suffering is nothing like He suffered for us. Keep Him in your heart and see what a difference He can make in your lives. I love Him with all of my heart and soul and wish for you the same comfort that I have found."

CHARLES ASKING FOR PEOPLE TO COME TOGETHER IN FRIENDSHIP AND UNDERSTANDING:

"Lets write about my inability to want to do things socially and how I always feel that people are looking at me when I enter a room. This is foolish, I know, but it is very painful to me and I need help so that I can be more confident. Sometimes, when I enter a room I almost feel as though I may not be able to stay even though I need the companionship of my peers as well as other people. Since I am nonverbal, all of the confidence leaves me when I approach people in social situations and I desperately need to communicate.

If people could come up to speak to me and not just look at me, I might feel better about myself. Most people are so uptight when they approach the handicapped that they fail to reach out to us and make us feel more secure in our surroundings. If people could only realize that we are the same as they, then we could all relax and start to enjoy each others company, and happiness would come to all of us as we feel the companionship of one another and the love of friendship.

I feel that other speech impaired people must feel the same way I do. I hope my book allows us to understand one another better whether we are handicapped or not. I hope that my book is successful in creating a new understanding for the growing need for all people, handicapped or not, to relate and help each other through life. It will be a wonderful experience for all of us to love one another and help each other in our journey through life. Life is so short so we must learn to take time to be in touch with our friends and family. Please think about this and lets make an effort to exchange our feelings and become friends."

CHARLES DISCUSSING RELATIONSHIPS:

"I would like to say to everyone that I am lonely for my peers and I hope that people without handicaps will remember to include us in their conversations. We nonverbal, autistic people are intelligent and would like to join in your conversations.

Please make an effort to approach us without being afraid that you will offend us if we are unable to answer. We are so anxious to be included in your conversations.

My own relatives have been unable to approach me and that has disturbed me to no end. They seem to think that I am an inanimate object and that I am not intelligent enough to speak to. I feel bad about this and would like to say to them that I love them and would want their friendship They are welcome in my home anytime and I hope, when they read this, that they will know not to reject me. I am a good person and I hold no animosity of any kind for their reluctance to approach me. Please remember that appearances don't always tell about the person inside. We need your understanding and love.

I think that perhaps people would be more comfortable with us if we could be allowed to speak to them through facilitated communication, first, and then they can see that we are intelligent and only wish to be able to converse intelligently about any and all subjects. I know I have always longed to talk about so many subjects but it is so difficult for people to approach me with any kind of a conversation from which I can learn. I think that I am intelligent enough to discuss almost anything. Please remember that we wish to be considered a part of society and not just people who are second class citizens."

CHARLES SPEAKING ABOUT EVENTS
IN HIS LIFE:

"I thought my trip tyo louisville. kentucky, was great, and i had a marvelous time at our friends'home.we ate there and then wsent to the rasces at churchill downs. daddy and bill spoo played the horses and we had a wonderful time. i am anxious togoback again, as i need to be with friends as a part of my rehabilityation is social interaction with people.my mother and father are wonderful to me, but i need other people in my life to make my life complete. our friends, the davises, and ourfriends, the clems make my life more enjoyable. i need to be able to communiate with more people, and then i can be more norma and less autistic. my friend.steve beck, and my friend, nancy bagatell, have helped me to reach out to others and be less isolated. i love them for their friendship and will never forget what they are doing for me. my friend,lynne vanevera, at the workshop, and my friend julie hayes also help me to adjust to being nonverbal, and i love them for it. of course i will alwaysd be indebted to susan utt and to vera pistel for their friendship. susan was responsible for my breakthrough on facilitated communication, and vera helped me to learn how to unbuckle my seatbelt, when we were in the developmental center at the workshop.

i am now very optimistic about robert romagna's bringing facilitated communiation into the workshop program for tyhe first time. he is a very fine man, and i love him for giving our cause every chance to reach the public and be instrumental in helping other nonverbal autistic people and others in need of a form of mcommunication. i am anxious to communicate with my friends, evan reed and david lubey, and ohters in the future. i would be remiss if i did not mention leona weatherholdt and the now deceased rose jackson for all of the patient, loving help and care they have given me over the years.

i feel so much better about the future, in spite of my extreme handicap, as i have my standby guardians, connie and cecil clem whom i love dealy. i hope my mother and fasther live for many years to come, but wwhen god calls them home, i will have my firends, connie and cecil to stand by me with their loving concern. for this i will always be grafteful. my breakthrough on facilitated communicaton has changed my life and the lives of so many others. i hope that it iss just a matter of time before there are no skeptcis in the world. it is our only hope for a meaningful, productive life"

CHARLES SPEAKING WITH MOTHER,
FEBRUARY 16, 1996

"You are so sweet to me mother dear that i would like to write you a poem, so here goes.

        you are my b heart and soul
        you are my soul and life to me
        i love you more tjan life itself
        and would love you even after death
        my darling mother dear
        you have always been by my side
        and you never tire of me
        i shall always be your little boy
        even though i am all grown up
        i think you live to make me happy
        and i live to love you too
        i i will always keep you in my heart throuhh
        all eternity."

MOTHER'S DAY PRESENT:

"I got you a Mother's Day present, but you can't open it until Mother's Day. I picked it out myself and hope you will like it as I love you more than life itself. I wanted you to have something from me alone as I have never been able to tell you how much I love you before. You have been the best mother in the whole world to me and Daddy and I love you more than you will ever know. I hope you like it, but if you don't you can return it. I hope you do like it as it reminds me of you. I thought the color was right as well as the style which I thought you would like. I think it will go well with the decor of the house."

Your son,
Charles"

(Mother's note: It seems that Charles was very good at keeping secrets as his gift was perfume.)

MOTHER'S DAY POEM FROM CHARLES
(as typed by Charles)to mother,

giving you tghis opoem for mothers dayt izssx very pas,k piea

hard for mde because rhewrs   there are no worsddss gopoop;

good enough to thganlk you for thre wsay ykou hawve deduj

kindly takejn care of me alll, of these years.

giving me hope

givibng med lobve

givibbng me hAppiness

giving me a viki vkko voicde to tell the woyrld tgu how much i

god looves uus.

just knkow that i love yikuj you so .

  lov, cbhy charl.esw

"Giving you this poem for Mother's Day is very hard for me because there are no words good enough to thank you for the way you have kindly taken care of me all of these years -

Giving me hope,
Giving me love,
Giving me happiness,
Giving me a voice to tell the world how much God loves us.
Just know that I love you so.
Love,
Charles"

CHARLES SPEAKING ABOUT HIS SOCIAL PROGRESS
10/25/97:

"this week i went to two parties and my thoughts about m y experience should be told i orderthat others like me will know not to gve up on their feelings of inadequacy in social occasions. o had a good time at both of thse parties and felt less frustrated than in the pst.i even danced with several friends and i as beginning to get the feel, of the rhythm when dancong. i love each and everyone of my friends for taking th timed to try to make me feel at ease. when i cme back to my residence i couldn't get to slep because i felt so great about feelingbetter in a social situation and being able to dance and eat. i want to tell other handicapped people to stand up proud and try to overcome their feelings of inadquacy as people are basicly kind and we need to have more relationships to help us overcome our insecurities."

CHARLES SPEAKING ABOUT THE RAPPORT
BETWEEN THE SPEAKER AND THE FACILITATOR IN
FC, 3/14/98:

"i would like to tell parents an educators that there are several factors that might come into play when the speaker will not communicate with tbe facilitator. first, i think that there must be a feeling of comfort on the part of the speaker. then there must be confidence o the part of the facilitator. the speaker doesn't want to feel like thn facilitator is testing his intelligence and is skepticAl about fc. then, the reason that some children may not speak with the parents is because they are so convinced that the parents are not really believing that fc does work and they may ferl as if they are making tjeir parents do something in which they don't rally bel.ike ve.then i alzso think that ut takezs time to get the right feel between the speaker and the facilitator. don'y give up. it is so importatnt to the child or adult to beable to comm unicate with others. it is terribletobe isolateddx and im]risoned."

Chapter Eight

Charles' Friend, Lincoln Grigsby

JOAN MARIAH AND HER SON, LINCOLN GRIGSBY:

During our trip to the 1996 Conference on Facilitated Communication in Syracuse, New York, my family and I met Ms. Joan Mariah. Joan and her son, Lincoln Grigsby, live in Fairfax, California. Lincoln is a 37 year old man who is autistic and nonverbal. The following accounts of his breakthrough on facilitated communication and how it has changed his life are given first by Joan and then by her son, Lincoln, who speaks by facilitated communication:

"In February of 1992 a TV program called Prime Time Live did a segment on something called 'Facilitated Communication'. I did not see it, but several friends excitedly told me about it, and I was given a couple of video-tapes of it. Before I saw the tape I was fearful as well as skeptical. Throughout the past 25 or so years there had been innumerable well-intentioned but worthless or even harmful treatments or techniques to deal with autism. However, after seeing the video program, I was deeply moved that these non-verbal autistic kids were finally getting to voice who they were. I telephoned and found out that in a couple of weeks there was going to be a training in our area. I contacted the organizers of this training and was told that all the training slots were filled and that they wouldn't put Link's name on a waiting list because it was already too lengthy. I asked them to indulge me and put Link's name on there, anyway, please. They did.

Lincoln Grigsby

At that time Link was 31 years old and had four people working with him part-time. Each of them viewed the video-tape and was interested. I was going through agonies of hope and doubt in the meantime. This poor young man had already been guinea-pigged to death, and I was afraid to subject him to one more thing. What if he couldn't do it? What if our expectations were too much pressure? What if it was a bogus happening? On the other hand, while we were watching the video-tape with Lincoln, one of the staff asked him if he thought FC was valid. Link shocked us all by verbally shouting "YES!" Also, just to look in Lincoln's eyes is to know that there is a depth of intelligence there, thoughts, feelings...all the accouterments of humanity with the encumbrances of atypical behavior and no speech.

The day arrived, February 19 (which Link was later to type was 'when he had been born'). True to my hunch, we'd been called the night before to fill one slot that had opened up. All of us attended the workshop and the one hour training appointment. On the way to the session I went into wreck-mode again and tried to assure Link that it was O.K. if this didn't work for him, etc., etc. I was so excited and at the same time fearful that it's embarrassing to remember. Link listened patiently, and then after we sat in the car going through my disclaimers intended to protect his self-esteem, he smiled, reached over and removed the car-keys, jumped out of the car, and headed for the building. He could hardly wait. We all crowded into the tiny room to receive the training. Our wildest hopes were surpassed, and the tears flowed. Link let us know who he was in that hour, and thanked us for the love and support we had given him. The trainer who was teaching us had never met any of us before, didn't know any of our names, and certainly not the rather unusual spelling of two of the names which Lincoln typed out. There have never been five more ecstatic people in one tiny space than in that hour. We still watch the video from time to time.

Six years have passed and although Link wants to be an 'independent typer' (one who needs no support for the pull-back of his typing arm) he hasn't made it yet. It is still a goal. My expectation since he now had a way to express himself, all our troubles were over, and that he'd just type-type-type was naive. As he pointed out, when you share who you are, there's a lot of responsibility. He had no responsibilities in his life before. We had not had a clue as to who he really was and our relationships to him were almost 100% projection. He also had power issues, self-esteem troubles, trust gaps, rage, and a life-long habit of not speaking out. He's struggled manfully to overcome these obstacles and I admire him greatly for his growth in all of these areas.

Lincoln's insights, ability to reason through difficulties, and his genuine spiritual acumen are remarkable. His violent behavioral outbursts have ceased. He still occasionally goes into sensory overload (a symptom of autism) but manages to control himself. Before FC, no amount of behavior modification or other interventions were effective and he had been ejected from the group home he had been in with a recommendation for State Hospital placement. He is making changes in his outlook, behavior, communication and socialization month by month. He has a growing circle of real friends who respect and admire him, and each passing month his trust in himself and others grows. He is trying to break old attitudinal habits and open himself up more to love. In other words, he is handling a lot of issues with which most of us struggle, with many additional disabilities that the rest of us don't have to contend with. Ironically, he is a non-verbal person who has a gift with words. He says he will probably never become verbal, but now he knows that he has a future, because he has gifts that he can share with others. He also types that he is more happy all the time, and that he knows he is making progress in his emotional development. He continues to astound and delight us and teach us. So far he has typed extensively with sixteen different people.

I, also, have had to go through some intense personal work and growth to break my old habits and attitudes of protecting him and 'mothering' him. As he says, 'old habits are hard to break, but it can be done, one step at a time'. I'm still taking one step after another, and it's a joyful journey. I will always be grateful to the Adriana Foundation and Doug Biklen of Syracuse University for enabling my son's life to expand by bringing us Facilitated Communication. And I am grateful to Lincoln for being the beautiful soul that he is."

ON NOVEMBER 27, 1996, CHARLES' FRIEND, LINCOLN GRIGSBY, MADE THE FOLLOWING COMMENTS FOR OUR BOOK. HE SPEAKS THROUGH FACILITATED COMMUNICATION:

"I AM A NON-VERBAL AUTISTIC MAN. EVER SINCE I CAN REMEMBER AS A CHILD I HAVE KNOWN THAT I AM AN INTELLIGENT HUMAN BEING WHO HAS HIS OWN IDEAS ABOUT HOW THINGS ARE IN THE WORLD.

I HAVE ALWAYS KNOWN THAT I HAD A CONTRIBUTION TO MAKE IN THE WORLD BUT AS A NON-VERBAL IN A VERBAL SOCIETY IT HAS BEEN VERY HARD UNTIL FACILITATED COMMUNICATION WHEN I BECAME FREE. I WAS GIVEN A WAY TO EXPRESS MYSELF TO THE WORLD.

YOU CANNOT KNOW HOW THIS FEELS TO FINALLY BE FREE TO EXPRESS WHO YOU ARE IN THE WORLD. PEOPLE CAN KNOW WHO YOU ARE AND YOU CAN BEGIN TO TALK TO OTHERS AND SHARE YOUR IDEAS AND LET PEOPLE KNOW WHAT YOU WANT IN LIFE.

YOU HAVE CONTROL OVER YOUR LIFE AND WHERE IT IS GOING FOR THE FIRST TIME EVER. NOW I CAN MAKE MY OWN DECISIONS ABOUT WHAT HAPPENS IN MY LIFE. BEFORE FC I COULD NOT EXPRESS WHAT I WANTED FOR MY LIFE AND PEOPLE DID NOT KNOW. NOW I HAVE A WAY TO TELL THEM.

MY FRIENDS ARE NOW ABLE TO TALK TO ME AND MANY OF THEM ARE HAPPY BECAUSE I CAN GIVE THEM ADVICE WHICH HAS REALLY HELPED THEM IN THEIR TIMES OF NEED. WE ALL NEED HELP SOMETIMES. FC HAS HELPED ME AND BECAUSE OF FC I AM ABLE TO HELP MY FRIENDS. ANOTHER NICE THING ABOUT FC IS THAT NOW WHEN I GO OUT I CAN LET PEOPLE KNOW MY IDEAS AND FEELINGS AND WHAT I WANT. THIS IS VERY HELPFUL.

AS THE POST ON MY DOOR SAYS "NOT BEING ABLE TO SPEAK IS NOT THE SAME AS NOT HAVING ANYTHING TO SAY". I HAVE ALWAYS HAD SOMETHING TO SAY AND WITH FC I FINALLY HAVE A WAY TO SAY IT. I HOPE ALL AUTISTICS WHO DO NOT TALK ARE ABLE TO FINALLY SPEAK WITH FC. WE HAVE ALOT TO TELL THE WORLD ABOUT HOW OUR

REALITY IS AND HOW IT IS DIFFERENT FROM OTHERS. IT LETS PEOPLE KNOW THAT THERE ARE MANY DIFFERENT WAYS TO SEE THE WORLD AND THE MANY DIFFERENT WAYS ARE WHAT MAKES LIFE INTERESTING. LIFE IS ALWAYS TRYING TO EVOLVE AND BE DIFFERENT. IT IS ALWAYS CREATING DIFFERENCE WHICH MEANS THAT THERE IS EVEN MORE TO LOVE.

I SOMETIMES SAY THIS WITH MY POEMS. BEFORE FC I WAS NOT ABLE TO WRITE MY POEMS BUT THE WORDS WERE IN MY HEAD, READY TO BE EXPRESSED. FC HAS HELPED ME TO DO THAT. WORDS CAN BE WAYS OF EXPRESSING OUR CARE AND LOVE FOR EVERYTHING. WHEN YOU ARE NON-VERBAL WORDS ARE AMAZING THINGS. WITH FC I AM ABLE TO COMMUNICATE WITH THESE AMAZING THINGS AND COMMUNICATE MY LOVE FOR ALL LIFE IN MY OWN SPECIAL WAY."

Note: In March 1993, Lincoln asked (via FC) to move alone to the studio apartment below his Mom's house. It would be the first time in his life that he would have time alone for more than half an hour at a time. We all were anxious because there was no precedent for this, but we also felt that it was a very important growth step for Lincoln and that he could do it. Lincoln also had some fears and doubts, and one day this poem poured out:

MY MOVE

MY MOVE KEEPS COMING
MY INDEPENDENCE IS FEARFULLY CLOSE AT HAND
READY TO BEGIN MY NEW LIFE ALONE
STRANGE TO FEAR WHAT I HAVE LONGED FOR SO LONG
KEEP MY PLACE IN YOUR HEART
JOIN ME IN MY NEW FOUND FREEDOM
LIFE IS EACH DAY
ONE STEP AT A TIME
I'LL TRUST MY SELF TO FEEL THIS GROWING PAIN
AND SURVIVE
READY TO CRAWL, READY TO FLY
REALLY READY, REALLY AFRAID.

(Facilitated February 19, 1993)

Chapter Nine

Hope for the Future

CHARLES SPREADS HIS WINGS

By an unexpected twist of fate, in the Spring of 1997, the Hale family was faced with a family trauma by Martel's sudden critical illness. Our secure little world almost crumbled in the tumultuous onslaught of fears and lifestyle changes which were to take place in the weeks that followed. Between April and July, Martel spent seven weeks in the hospital with an infection in his blood stream, resulting in open-heart surgery with a mitral valve repair and a six-way bypass, all of this at the age of 74. Our prayers were answered and, thanks to a fine staff of doctors at the Winchester Medical Center, Martel returned home approximately three weeks after surgery.

In the meantime, about a week after his father entered the hospital for the first time, Charles was placed in respite care at Grafton School in order that I might be free to spend as much time at the hospital as was needed. During the last few years, it had really taken both his father and me, working together as a team, to meet the daily needs of our son. We had planned to keep Charles at home for as long as we were able to care for him. That is what we both had always wanted to do. When Charles was able to communicate with us and make his wishes known through the use of FC, he had told us that he would like to remain at home as long as it was possible. His father and I were delighted as that is exactly what we wanted to hear!

We have always been a close knit family and, as such, our greatest fear and concern was what would happen to Charles when we were no longer alive or able to physically and mentally care for him. With the onset of Martel's illness, something which was almost too painful to think about had taken place. Charles was no longer in the bosom of his family and his flight toward a more independent way of life had begun. A few weeks after he entered his respite care at Grafton, he told us that he was then 40 years old and needed to become more independent while his father and I were still here to help with the emotional adjustment of leaving home; therefore, he made the request that we allow him to remain in residence permanently. Charles had rationalized that it would be best for him to make the adjustment then, in a living situation in which he was happy, than to have to experience the trauma of another adjustment in the future, at a time when he might also be confronted with the loss of one or both of his parents. The following description of his adjustment to living away from home for the first time in his life was typed by Charles, via the technique of FC, without the correction of typographical errors:

"when i found that my father was so seriously ill and was going to have open heart surgery i knew that my mother needed to be with him and that is when i realized tht she needed complete freedom from caring for me for the first time in my life.she had always been therfe for me all my life, but now she was needed with daddy.i went to the group home and i found that it was best as i am forty years old and need to prepare myself for survival when my parents are gone and i am left without my support system both physically and mentally.i think that a child needs the support of his parents as long as they are young and in golod health, but when they begin to age it is time for them to think of becoming independende3nt even though it is difficult to break the ties.my trip to the group home was the most traumatic thing in my life. when i arrived there is wasx in shock because i felt lost without my parents.it was an experience that i will always remember and i would like to share how i felt.i was in shock for the first few hours but as the days went on i discovered that i could survive and that the staffwas wonderful andt eally cared about me and the other people in residdnce.they found out about my needs and took iy from thefre.they are the most dedicated people in their caring for the disabled and treat us with respect and as adults.

this de3dication by staff was not an entirely new experiencefor me as i experienced the same dedication as a child and adult in an ahrc school program in newyork city for many years and now at the norywestern workshop here in winchester, virginia.i would also l9ke to telk you about the fact that my residentialstaff atgrafton is currently trying to learn to communicate with me through facilitated communiation and tjeyare doing a good job, because tjeyhave never done facilitation with othwr people and have just recewntly received workshop training at grafton.i love each and everyone of them more than i can say. to be locked away for so many years i can appreciate this effort more than a person could believe unlwess they have spent most of their life trying to make people understand thatthey arefe intellent an havethe same needs and desires as other people.god bless all of the people who have and still are trying to bring some happiness into our lives.i wouldalso like to tell the reader of this book about my inability to o simple movement practices independently things like dressing, andshaving and bathing and even wiping myself.i have mentioned this earlier in our book, but wish to elaborate more on the fact that even being away fromhome i am still unable to accomplish these things, so i attribute this to the facat that my apraxia and movement disturbance is something tnati maynever recover from.i know that parentsworry about the quality of care providers other tyhan themselves, but i want to encourage you to know that there are good people oin the world who care enough about you to try their besto help youj with these self help skills. i miss my parents very much all week, but thjen i can come home often and this carries me through the week.my parents areso loving that it will stay with me all my life andallow me to know that i am a very fortunate individual ddspite my handicap a worthwhile person who will go through life trying to bring kindness and love to others like myself and those less fortunate ones of whom there are many. not everyone has had a good support system all of their lives and therefore must have help from otjers.if i could talk i would like to be a ministerf and thank god for my blessings which are many in spite of my handic ap."

When I asked Charles if he would like me to send the above message to his residential staff on Packer Street, here in Winchester, he replied as follows: "i think that ould be great and it would allow them to know that i appreciate them more than i can say. tjey are my angels here on earth and i want them to know how i feel about them. you send all o have said as i want them to know how i llove them all. i think that my housemates are special too and i love them too.they have become my friends and i think we are very compatible. i hope we can remain togdther a long time. this is important to me in that i need friends and we get aong so wedll."

Charles has been living away from home for over a year now and continues to slowly improve in some of the self-help skills about which he has spoken. He is gaining in self-confidence in social engagements and in new experiences and surroundings. He still has a long way to go to complete his dream of life; but, despite the great handicap with which he struggles each day, he continues to amaze and inspire us with his courage and great heart. It is evident that he is spreading his wings as if to fly. "Take off, sweet boy, into brighter tomorrows!"

Sensory Overloads, Frustrations, Anxieties and Special Gifts

" I would like to explain how my eyesight is different from other people who do not have neurological problems. When I see an object, it comes through in a shattered glass effect and I often cannot look for any length of time as it is hard for me to see without pain. I think that we are more inclined to be nervous as we see things in such a distorted form. We do not always have to see what we are doing and that is one reason that we don't want to look at the keyboard. Please understand that we are trying to look but our nervous system will not always allow us to focus. I am anxious to get help for I need to work toward independence. I mean that we see through our peripheral vision not only in typing but in focusing on other objects as well. I believe that peripheral vision is acute to make up for the fact that our straight forward vision is impaired. We need help. When I say that we see in shattered glass effect I do not mean all the time, but most of the time our vision is impaired to some degree. We need someone to be able to remedy this as did Tom Page in obtaining his glasses which have prisims. I feel that we

82

autistic people are intelligent in most cases and that is why we are so nervous and impatient in getting our messages out. We are inclined to see things on the ground which come into our faces as big bolders and holes that we look into. If there were boulders and holes, we would fall into them and be killed. I hope that you will believe what I say about this problem as we need your understanding and help in showing other people why we are so different than they are. I believe that anyone with this problem will respond with many mannerisms which a person without the particular impairment will not understand. When we are calm, we do not see as many of these kinds of visual exaggerations or defects as we do when we are having overloads to the nervous system. When we go to sleep, we are at rest, and then only, as we are upset most of our waking hours. When I am calm, I can concentrate on learning; but, when I have overloads, I can do very little to function normally. All our overloads are triggered by electrical impulses being sent from the brain and one can do nothing to control them when they start. They come without warning but most often when one is tired or stressed out by someone or something. I am so anxious to learn and get on with my life that this probably causes more overloads than before. I seem to be having more all of the time because I am getting older and feel that time is running out to get things done that I very much would like to accomplish while I am still young and able.

When I recently went to see an eye doctor and then my dentist, I was embarrassed that I could not cooperate, but my overloads were worse than ever and I acted like a baby and not as the intelligent man that I feel that I am. My overloads come in the form of visual and hearing distortions. This, of course, only occurs at the time of any overload occurence. There is also a sensitivity to a hot or cold object. Everyone has this at times, but I have it most always when I am having an overload with regard to my hearing and sight as well. Someone can help us at this time by being patient, speaking in a lower voice and giving us encouragement to keep our morale up as this time of an overload is greater than one can possibly believe, with all of the above sounds, feelings and distortions coming into play. I hope

83

that someday more people will understand and support in all aspects of our lives. This is why I want to get an education and help people like me have a fuller, more comfortable life rather than a life of stress and depression.

I think that I need help in finding someone who understands the neurological problems of autism. I would be willing to try to tell the doctor what my problems are. I have such overloads most of the time that it is difficult to keep my sanity. I see things in exaggerated forms and hear in intensified volume. It is hard to keep one's mind focused on a task. In overloads one has other factors which come into play like color changes from time to time. I don't mean normal changes in color, but I am referring to color exaggerations which come during times of stress when one is having overloads. These come much more often now when I get stressed out by frustration in not being able to do facilitated communication with everyone I wish to communicate with. Since my breakthrough I want to speak now that I know people realize that I have a good mind. I need to feel the confidence of the facilitator. I feel their lack of confidence because I know that they are learning. I hope that people will start training staff again. I would like to say that a day without facilitated communication is like imprisonment all over again and you must understand that I need help.

Sounds most of the time are very loud and this, of course, disturbs my nervous system. I have always thought that I needed sensory perception therapy as it is frustrating to hear sounds so amplified. This only comes about when an overload occurs. Also, I have a sensitivity to touch and an example of this is when I touch someone or something and get an electrical shock.

I think that another thing I might mention is that when one tries too hard to do a particular task, he may find that his overloads become more acute and then he is back to where he began. This might apply when I am unable to see something and bring it back upon command. If I get overly anxious, it may not be possible to see whatever I am looking for. This, in turn causes one to think that I am not understanding. If my mother asks me to bring something to the table, for instance, I may be unable to see it as I am anxious to prove myself. Then, when can't find the object, I feel depressed. It would be helpful if the person making the request could speak in a lower voice and perhaps make the handicapped person feel less frustrated in his attempt to comply to the request. Then everyone feels better about the fact that he is less frustrated and more confident. We are so self conscious in our inabilities that we feel less than capable many times.

I would like to tell the reader how I learned to add and subtract without lessons. First of all, I started listening to people talk about adding and subtracting. Then I heard a television program on adding and subtracting and they gave examples of how one carried the numbers to the next column. I started practicing in my head and when my mother asked me to add and subtract, I found that I could do so. I had always thought about adding and subtracting as a means of occuping my time. Then when Vera Pistel and even earlier teachers showed examples on the board, I listened and tried to add and subtract in my leisure. Then I heard a program on multiplying and started practicing. I still do this very often to keep from being nervous in overloads. I could pass basic arithmetic, I believe, even without being able to write. I have a proclivity for mathematics, I believe.

I will try to explain to the reader how I am able to type without looking, In the first place, we have a gift of sight which allows us to see and focus with peripheral vision. When we are not focusing, we are remembering the letters in our minds. We learned the keyboard rapidly as we have an ability to see at great lengths and in a wide variety of different focuses, some of which are very difficult for other people to see as we have an extra sense which allows us to do this very quickly. I hope this begins to allow people to understand our way of learning. This also applies as to how we learn in other circumstances.

I believe that when one loses a sense such as speech, he also gains another sense which allows him to see and also learn rapidly. I mean that we have very good memories and can grasp something in a short length of time. This might be why people think that we are not really doing the speaking. It is an unbelievable gift for people to understand, but I am telling the truth to you. I hope that you will take this at face value and begin to allow us to be helped.

I think that my overloads are more frequent now as I need to get on with my life and I also worry about my mother and father getting older. I know that losing one's parents is normal, but I am handicapped and need the support of my family more than if I were a person without problems. They are my life. I know that I will be able to go on in life, but my life will never be the same for me. I am a very people oriented person, but being nonverbal keeps me isolated to a large degree. I need to get my education and show the skeptics that I am real and need to be working to help others in their fight to be heard.

I have been learning all my life, as I have mentioned before, but this is difficult for anyone who is verbal to understand because we appear to be incapable of learning as our whole appearance defies this. We are so neurologically impaired that we look as if we are incapable of understanding. If people will only stop doubting us, then we can move on with our lives. If a handicapped person gives up, they are giving up on life and they need encouragement in doing their best to live up to their potential whatever it may be. I know that I am getting older and I need to do something in life that makes my life worth living and my future promising.

I would like very much to be able to lecture and advise parents and professionals in the field as I have a great desire to do something in life for all of the other disabled people like myself. They need to be understood and I have experience which I believe is invaluable. I know how frustrating it is to do and teach others to do what they would be happy in accomplishing for themselves. I have longed to help others from the time I was a youngster. I have much love in my heart. I feel that if one has love to share with others,

that is perhaps the greatest gift that one could give in life. I would like to teach people to hold their heads up high and not fall into the habit of thinking that they are not valuable individuals and need to give up and vegetate.

I need my parents' help in acting as ambassadors of my cause. They care more about me than anything else in their life and I am fortunate to have a good support system. My staff is also a fine support system as are my standby guardians, Connie and Cecil Clem. I have been fortunate in spite of my extreme handicap. I hope that other people will help us nonverbal people to realize our dreams. We have the same dreams of success and happiness that normal people do."

MY PROJECTIONS FOR THE FUTURE

my projections for the future

"i think that if i can get my ged and get all of the education i can, i will be able to help other people to do as much with their ;ives as they are able to without having to spend an entire lifvetime in absolute vegetation and desperayion as time goes so quickly and then we are too old to take advantage of what opportunities prevail themselves to us. i know that i would nbe a good teacher if i could gey enough educatikon to pursue my field whichwould be in the field of developmental disability. i would liketo give people hope for thefuture as i am an example of a person witj a lifelong disability who has bene able to learn much of whatg i know through observation and a fdesire to learn. many people don.t appl the,msrlves and wast their lives thinking about toomany unimportant things and not concentrating on things that will enable them to accomplish what they would like to oin their lives. one must have some kind of a plan even though they atr disabled as life is meant to be lived as well as posible. i hope that people will help me to livesa more productive life and help otjers as i love people and wold like to spend my remaining days in a productive way. in order to do tjis, i am asking people on my staff to please try to learn to do facilitated communication with me and thus allow me to reach my goals in life. i am deeply indebtedx to all of the people who are working to make my life better. god blesds them all. i hope that this will not put too much extra work on their shoulders."

A LIGHT AT THE END OF THE TUNNEL

The time and devotion involved in caring for a severely disabled child sometimes might be compared to having a new baby every year and then some. It can be exhausting and emotionally draining for everyone in the family and yet it can be the most rewarding experience in the life of a family. It takes a great deal of patience and love to survive the heartbreak it brings to a parent. The seeming loss of one's hopes and dreams of a normal life for a loved one can be devastating. Families can either fall apart or become stronger as time passes. Raising a so-called "normal" child is not easy; raising a disabled child is another dimension. How a family responds to the challenge depends upon its priorities and its ability to work together as a team. Some families become stronger and even flourish in the love which having a disabled child in the family entails; others are unable to withstand the constant care and sacrifice of time and attention to one's own needs which this may require.

Mary Jane and Martel (seated right) attending Grafton's Shenandoah Valley Advisory Board Meeting.

Some parents are not emotionally or physically able to care for a disabled child. They may have a child with a severe behavior problem; they may be struggling alone without a helpmate; it may be necessary for both parents to work; but, if the family structure is strong and if nothing is more important than caring for the family member who is the most needy, then somehow a family is sustained by this love and commitment and is willing and able to cope with almost anything.

Whether or not the child is able to remain at home, parents of a disabled child have a lifelong worry about this child, but, hopefully, life is improving and will continue to improve for many disabled people. The trend toward de-institutionalization, moving the disabled away from mere custodial care and into the community, where they may be more easily observed and properly cared for in a more homelike environment, seems to offer a better chance for their protection and happiness. The greatest fear for every parent of a disabled child is what might happen when they are no longer living or able to keep their child at home. Even when the child is leaving home for short-term rehabilitation in the best of environments, the worry is still there.

Charles is our only child. We perhaps have been more fortunate in one way than many other parents with larger families who have the need to divide their time and attention in other directions; however, we, too, did have other responsibilities. We are now in our seventies and are fortunate enough to still be able to provide a loving home for our son to return to on weekends and holidays. We have lived though the hyperactive, kicking, screaming, running away years which, fortunately, with Charles were never extreme enough to place him in the category of a "behavior problem." With the coming of the maturation process, he seemed to continue to improve with each passing year. With a new ability to communicate through facilitated communication, his progress has become more apparent.

We have not been perfect parents. Perhaps Charles might have been able to do more self-help skills if I had not done so many things for him, thinking that he was unable to learn more easily because of mental retardation; however, his father and I have always loved him every minute of every day...regardless! We parents can only do the best we can; but, whether a child remains at home with his parents, or is cared for by others who may also provide a good home for him in their efforts to help him, the most important thing we can do for a disabled child, or for any child, is to let him know that he is a worthwhile person who is loved more than anything in the world.

IN CONCLUSION

Although Charles Martel Hale, Jr. joyfully acknowledges that he now has "A Means To Shout," on March 27, 1996, while typing with his In-Home instructor, Stephen Beck, he poignantly expressed the one innate longing which still may remain in his heart forever. The following verse reveals this dream:

> "I hope to see the morning
> Every night before I sleep.
> The dream I have is never true;
> It is gone before I wake.
> I pray to see the morning
> When the voice inside me yells.
> I know the dream is in my head;
> I pray to sleep again."

Life is not easy; but, in the words of our son, "Whose life is ever perfect anyway?"

ADDENDUM

In April of 1998, a Qualitative Investigation of Movement Differences and Occupational Performance of an individual with Autism was submitted by Brett R. DeVore and Vasilia Kouloumbre in partial satisfaction of the requirements for the degree of Masters of Science in Occupational Therapy at Shenandoah University, in Winchester, Virginia. Their faculty advisor for the project, which began in the Fall of 1997, was Nancy Bagatell.

The above scholarly project was designed to investigate the impact of the movement differences on the occupational performance of an individual with autism. The participant in the study was Charles Hale (a.k.a. H.G.) who had attended the Northwestern Workshop, in Winchester, Virginia for a period of 17 years. Charles, who has a movement/planning disorder, was identified as exhibiting movement differences by his Occupational therapist, Nancy Bagatell.

Charles was videotaped in his work setting five times in a period of three months. He communicated via facilitated communication on a laptop computer. The taping lasted 15 to 20 minutes and he was interviewed following the work sessions for approximately one hour. The researchers used guiding questions for the interviews, but also relied on the development of questions in regard to movement during that particular work session. An additional interview took place outside the workplace for approximately one hour. The interviews following the work sessions were videotaped and transcribed by the researchers. The analysis of the data led to two main themes, that of getting stuck and unstuck. The human components were The Three S's: Starting, Stopping and Switching. The researchers observed that Charles displayed specific movement difference patterns and particularly exhibited difficulties starting, continuing and switching a motion.

The following comments by Charles in answer to questions by the researchers are shown to provide the reader a further understanding of Charles' disability. His words have been corrected for spelling and typographical error content:

The researchers stated that Charles often appears with his eyes squinted and he is rarely seen with his eyes opened. When asked about why his eyes are usually closed, he responded, "I close my eyes on days my lids don't stay open. I get tired by the light. It is hard to keep up." On one occasion, Charles stated, "I lose the feel of where my body is. It is like forgetting just how I plan to move. You give me plenty to think over...like why I get stuck. I'll tell you it is hard to understand why the brain makes mistakes." In the same interview, Charles reported, "It is funny to think that I get stuck and can't move by myself. I'm thinking that my face gets stuck." He went on to explain that "I can't always laugh or cry properly...people think I'm all serious, but I like humor." In discussing what helps Charles get unstuck, he stated, "touch in general, but I need time to organize." He elaborated by stating: "It (needing time to organize) means that it is time to put things together. Time is needed because my brain is different. It means that thoughts and movement have to be put together." When asked to elaborate when things are harder to be put together, Charles replied, "I think it is based on how the brain is in gear."

During an interview session, Charles began to type about facilitated communication and he stated, "I need the support of a facilitator to get the rhythm...I think that I just don't have rhythm." He was then asked if having the facilitator provides him with rhythm and he replied, "yes, but I am not sure how." When asked to elaborate on his comment, Charles stated, "I'm just getting this idea that the movement difference that I have might interfere with the typing. That is why understanding FC is hard for most people."

During one interview session, it was noted that Charles was getting tired and was asked if he wanted a break and he replied, "yes." He took a break and upon his return he initiated the discussion by stating, "I am thinking that it is interesting how my mind influences my body...I think that I am trying to tell my body to 'go.' I'm not too sure it works all the time." When asked what the things are that make his body 'go' if his mind can't, he replied, "Things like music and (his aide)." It was observed that Charles had some difficulties picking up some of the smaller objects. In the interview following the work session, Charles reported that the task today is more fun...it is harder but more stimulating. I need more help just because I am not very dexterous.)

Charles and I would like to take this opportunity to thank the Shenandoah University students, Brett and Vasilia, who were kind enough to allow us to use the above excerpts from their study as an addendum to our book, thereby allowing another dimension of Charles' bird's eye view into his life to be seen and understood.

As of May 1, 1998, Charles has left the Northwestern Workshop and is now a full time consumer at Grafton School. He is in the day training program as well as the residential facility, working toward more community inclusion.

AFTERWORD

One of Charles' pleas for help has been answered! Thanks to an agreement between our friend, Joan Mariah, and Michael McSheehan, a facilitated communication trainer from New Hampshire, who came to Winchester (April 1999) to work with Charles and his Grafton staff, Charles has now begun to focus and facilitate at the elbow level. The above mentioned fading is more conducive to Charles' future typing independence. We are extremely grateful for this help. He now types: "moving to independence. proud too."

TERMINOLOGY

THE ELUSIVE USE OF THE TERM "MENTAL" RETARDATION AS OPPOSED TO "FUNCTIONAL" RETARDATION

There are so many things that Charles is unable to do that might very well cause the uninformed person to consider him to be mentally retarded despite the cognition with which he speaks since his breakthrough on facilitated communication. Because of his extreme apraxia and movement disability, Charles or anyone else with a similar problem could quite easily be looked upon as mentally retarded because of their inability to perform certain seemingly simple tasks and respond to certain commands which a mentally cognizant individual would be expected to do.

The term 'retardation' in itself is an abnormal slowness of thought or action; whereas, the term 'mental retardation' refers to one's abnormal mental competence. I believe that Charles is therefore 'functionally' retarded but not 'mentally' retarded. There is a difference and in order for one to be able to more accurately understand and predict a disabled person's potential, we need to recognize the definition of functional as 'affecting physiological or psychological functions.' As Charles so aptly expresses it, "Appearances don't always count."

DEFINITION OF AUTISM

The following definition of Autism appeared in the Sept.-Oct. 1996 issue of the Newsletter of the Autism Society of America, Inc.:

Autism is a severely incapacitating life-long developmental disability that typically appears during the first three years of life. The result of a neurological disorder that affects functioning of the brain, autism and its behavioral symptoms occur in approximately fifteen out of every 10,000 births. Autism is four times more common in boys than girls. It has been found throughout the world in families of all racial, ethnic, and social backgrounds. No known factors in the psychological environment of a child have been shown to cause autism.

Some behavioral symptoms of autism include:

(1)   Disturbances in the rate of appearance of physical, social, and language skills.

(2)   Abnormal responses to sensations. Any one or a combination of senses or responses are affected: sight, hearing, touch, balance, smell, taste, reaction to pain, and the way a child holds his or her body.

(3)   Speech and language are absent or delayed, while specific thinking capabilities may be present.

(4)   Abnormal ways of relating to people, objects, and events.

Autism occurs by itself or in association with other disorders that affect the function of the brain, such as rival infections, metabolic disturbances, and epilepsy. It is important to distinguish autism from retardation or mental disorders since diagnostic confusion may result in referral to inappropriate and ineffective treatment techniques. The severe form of the syndrome may include extreme self-injurious, repetitive, highly unusual and aggressive behavior. Special educational programs using behavioral methods have proved to be the most helpful treatment for persons with autism.

Autism Is Treatable - Early diagnosis and intervention are vital to the future development of the child.

The Autism Society of America was organized in 1965 as the National Society for Autistic Children - NSAC. It is dedicated to the education and welfare of children and adults with severe disorders of communication and behavior.

WHAT IS APRAXIA AND HOW DOES IT RELATE TO VERBAL-AUDITORY AGNOSIA IN PERSONS WITH AUTISM DISORDER?

By Doris Allen, Associate Professor in Psychiatry
at the Albert Einstein College of Medicine
(excerpted from CSAAC Newsletter, Summer 1992)

First, it is important to understand that there are several types of apraxia. There is an apraxia which results in the inability to imitate the movement of others. There is an apraxia which prevents individuals from executing movements in response to verbal commands, and there is an apraxia which prohibits the individual from executing the proper movement when shown the real object (e.g., after being shown a toothbrush and toothpaste the individual cannot demonstrate how to use these objects even if he can brush his teeth spontaneously). There is also ideational apraxia in which the individual cannot execute movements to depict imaginary actions (such as if asked to demonstrate how to hammer a nail into a wall, the individual cannot pick up an imaginary nail, hammer, and demonstrate the hammering action). In addition to these motor apraxias, there is a verbal apraxia which prevents a person from consistently putting his ideas into oral language.

Some individuals with apraxia have a single apraxia, but they may have combinations of apraxia. We know this from research on adult patients with identified brain lesions. For an individual to require physical support from another human being, one would assume that the client had both a verbal apraxia and a problem with manual motor execution.

Clearly, there are children who do better with visual language than auditory language. That's because they can't process through the auditory system. Children who can learn language visually but not through the ear have a verbal-auditory agnosia, not a verbal apraxia. A lot of children and adults with autism have verbal-auditory agnosia and stay mute, without speaking their whole lives, but can use a visual system such as a language board, computers or sign language, and they can often learn to read and write. They do so without any support at all. If a person can use visual language but not the auditory/verbal language system, this is a sign that the auditory system is out, not the motor system. So when you teach these children to read and write they don't need support of the arm, unless they also have motor apraxia.

Not all individuals with autism have verbal agnosia, and not all have any form of apraxia. And there is no evidence that all individuals with autism who have verbal agnosia also have motor apraxia. It is possible to have neither, either alone, or both. There is a subset of individuals with autism who have verbal agnosia and motor apraxia, but there are also individuals with autism whose language impairments are due neither to verbal agnosia nor motor apraxia. Due to the variety of pathogenic mechanisms, it is naive at best to believe that there is a single method that can hope to remediate all individuals with autism.

MOVEMENT DISTURBANCE/DIFFERENCE

The following excerpts are taken from a publication by The Autism National Committee:

What is movement disturbance/difference?

This term refers to an interference in the efficient, effective use of movement which is not caused by paralysis or weakness, but by difficulties in the regulation of movement. Modern models of neuroscience include sensory perception in the term movement because the regulation of movement depends on sensory perception, and vice versa.

The word "difference" is included as a reminder that these regulatory challenges are not necessarily disturbing for the person who experiences them; problems may ensue when others have difficulty interpreting or responding to a person who moves differently, or when others are unaccepting of differences.

Why do movement differences occur? What is their connection to sensory regulation and perception?

The basis for the overlapping lists of behaviors labeled "autism" and "mental retardation" may be found in the brain's regulating or tracking systems for predicting sensory consequences of all types, and for relaying useful predictions to motor and other output systems. For example, when these tracking systems are not working reliably, the person may be unable to correctly estimate the "trajectory" of a stimulus and regulate an efficient response.

When these off-the-mark estimates are relayed to the body's motor systems, they produce movements which undershoot or overshoot the target, as well as disrupt the coordination of movement involved in social interaction. (This complex synchrony of body language and timing is often referred to as "the dance of relationships.")

When skewed estimates of a stimulus are relayed to the systems that regulate sensations, they produce analogous "undershoots" and "overshoots" (e.g. hyper-or hypo-sensitive hearing, vision, smell, touch; overreactions of "fight or flight"). Since action cannot be separated from perception, sensory regulatory problems also have a profound effect on the production and coordination of movements crucial to social interaction and communication.

What is the significance of movement in rethinking labels such as autism/ Pervasive Developmental Disorder and retardation?

Neuroscientists consider movement regulation and sensory regulation to be "two sides of the same coin." In fact it is not hard to imagine why individuals with movement disturbances would be seen to have difficulties in social communication and interaction, where even a small difference in behavior can have an enormous effect. Smiling too much or too late or at the wrong time, grimacing when you mean to grin, taking ten seconds rather than the expected two seconds to respond, all can give an enormous impression. If these problems begin early in life, obviously they will interrupt the person's ability to participate in "the dance of relationships." This interruption will further narrow the range of available learning experiences.

Focusing on symptoms of movement disturbance is not a way of adding a new label or adding new "deficits" to the lengthy lists already used to define disabilities such as autism and mental retardation. It is a way of moving beyond the judgmental, socially-defined elements of these lists and labels toward an understanding and appreciation of the nature of each person's experience.

What sorts of movement differences have been associated with people diagnosed with autism/PDD or mental retardation?

Movement differences are manifested in a wide range of behaviors, including the more easily-identifiable activities such as unusual gait and posture, constant physical movement, or repetitive rocking. Other movement differences tend to become evident at transition points. Among these are:

Starting - difficult initiating;

Executing - difficulty with the rate, rhythm, target, etc. of movement;

Continuing - difficulty "staying on track," not taking alternative paths, etc.;

Stopping - difficulty terminating a movement; the tendency to "perseverate"; getting "stuck" in one sensory mode like staring into space;

Combining - difficulty adding a sensory mode or a movement, e.g. listening to someone speak while watching their gestures and facial expression, doing two things at once, etc.;

Switching - difficulty "letting go" of one perception or movement and initiating a new one.

When there is an imbalance in the systems regulating movement, there may be a tendency for disruptions in other systems such as perception, emotion, and thought. These may include:

Difficulty "calling up" an emotion or finding the motivation needed for an action;

Having one's attention repeatedly drawn to some insignificant detail or event;

Not being able to initiate a request until someone else mentions it;

Getting stuck on a repetitive thought;

Difficulty in maintaining or letting go of a topic of conversation.

These difficulties often become evident during interactions where synchrony of movement, thought and emotion form the basis of relationship.

The above brochure was developed by Pat Amos (editor); Anne Donnellan, PhD; Mary Lapos; Martha Leary, MA CCC/SLP; Kathy Lissner-Grant; Ralph Maurer, MD; and Barbara Moran.

REFERENCES

Allen, Doris, Associate Professor in Psychiatry, Albert Einstein College of Medicine. (excerpted from CSAAC Newsletter, Summer 1992). What Is Apraxia And How Does It Relate To Verbal-Auditory Agnosia In Persons With Autism Disorder?

Autism National Committee. Amos, Pat (editor); Donnellan, Anne, PhD; Leary, Martha; MACCC/SLP; Lissner-Grant, Kathy; Maurer, Ralph, MD; and Moran, Barbara (Brochure) Movement Disturbance/Difference.

Autism Society of America. (1996) Issue of the Newsletter of the Autism Society of America, Inc. Definition of Autism.

Biklen, Douglas. (1992) Division of Special Education & Rehabilitation, Syracuse University, Syracuse, New York. Facilitated Communication.

Biklen, Douglas. (1993) Teachers College Press. Communication Unbound.

Biklen, Douglas and Cardinal, Donald N. (1997) Teachers College Press. Contested Words/Contested Science.

Crossley, Rosemary. (1994) Teachers College Press. Facilitated Communication Training.

Crossley, Rosemary. (1997) NAL/Dutton. Speechless.

DeVore, Brett and Kouloumbre, Vasilia. (1998) Movement Differences And Occupational Performance of an Individual with Autism: A Qualitative Investigation.

Donnellan, Anne and Leary, Martha. (1995) DRI Press. Movement Differences and Diversity in Autism/Mental Retardation

About the Authors

Mary Jane Hale is the author and primary facilitator for her son, Charles. The Hale family lived on Long Island, New York, for twenty-four years before moving to Winchester, Virginia, where they have resided for the past twenty years. The family moved to Virginia after Mary Jane's husband, Martel, a former Special Agent with the FBI, retired from the New York office.

Mary Jane and Martel have long been advocates of the mentally retarded and the developmentally disabled, both in New York and Virginia. The family recently received the ARC/NSV "Family of the Year" award. Mary Jane and Martel are currently serving on Grafton School's Shenandoah Valley Advisory Board in Winchester. They are now in their mid-seventies.

Co-author Charles Martel Hale, Jr. hopes to give the reader a "bird's eye view" of the world of a nonverbal man with autism. Being apraxic/dyspraxic, Charles had no way of expressing himself as the intelligent, extremely cognizant man he really is; hence, in Charles' own words, "I Had No Means To Shout!"

9 781585 004010